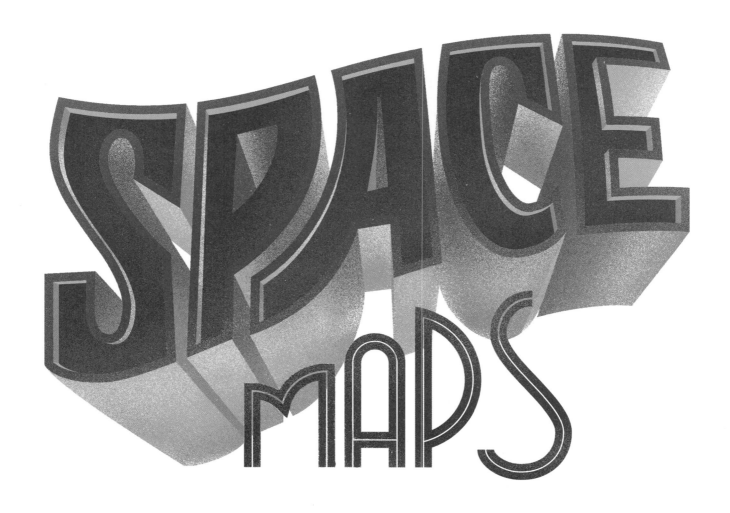

SPACE MAPS

LARA ALBANESE

ILLUSTRATED BY **TOMMASO VIDUS ROSIN**

What on Earth Books

CONTENTS

Mapping the Stars 4
The scientific map of the sky 6
The equatorial map of the sky 8
The Greek sky 10
The Chinese sky 12
The South African sky 14

Where Are We? 16
Galaxies 18
The Milky Way 20
The Sun 22
The solar system 24
Journeys through the solar system 26
The Earth 28
Light pollution 30
The Moon 32
Lunar explorations 34

What Are Other Planets Like? 36
Mercury, the Sun's neighbor 38
Venus, the dazzling planet 40
Mars, the red planet 42
Exploring Mars 44
Jupiter, the giant among planets 46
Jupiter's moons 48
Saturn, the lord of the rings 50

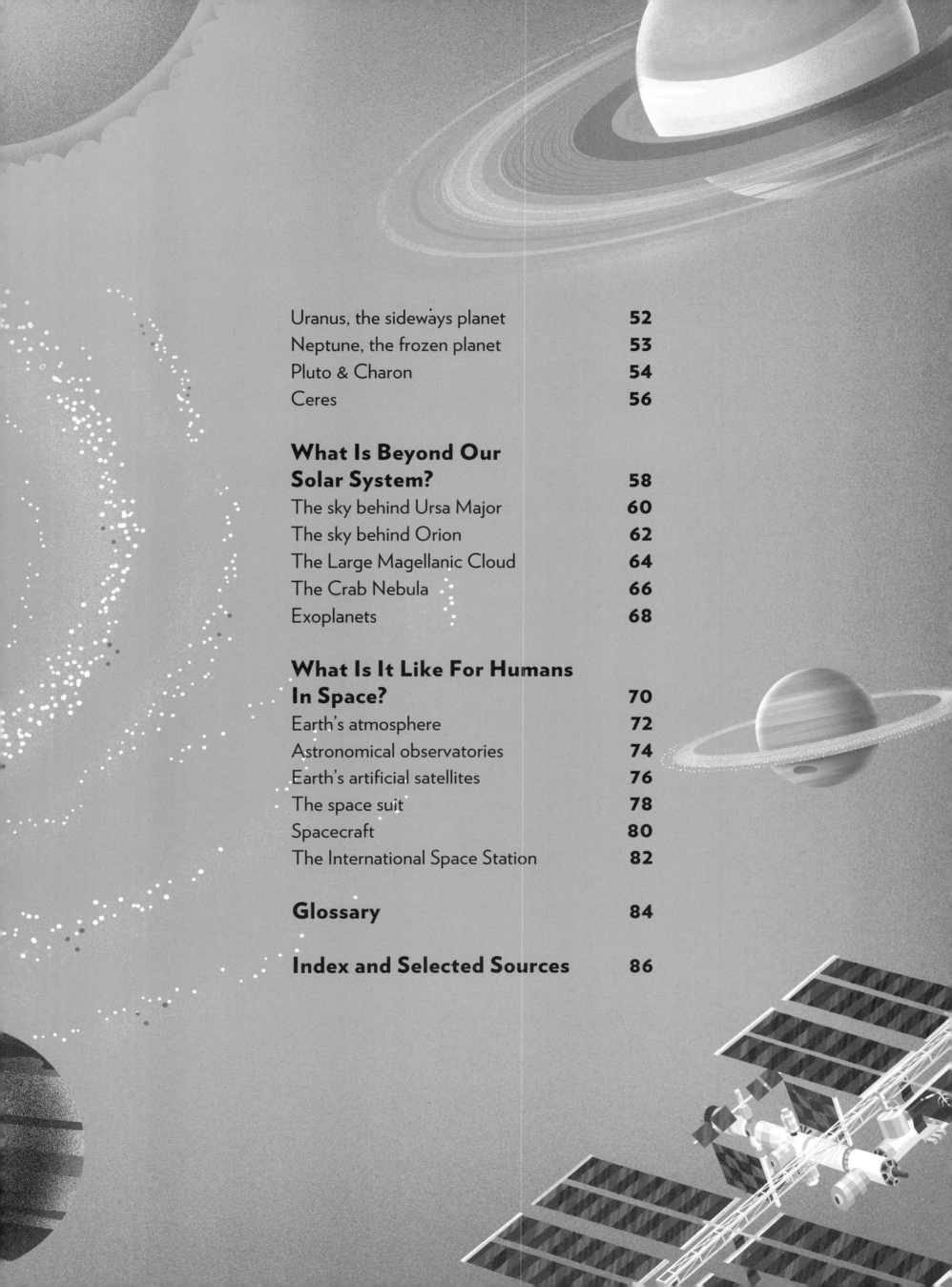

Uranus, the sideways planet   **52**
Neptune, the frozen planet   **53**
Pluto & Charon   **54**
Ceres   **56**

**What Is Beyond Our
Solar System?**   **58**
The sky behind Ursa Major   **60**
The sky behind Orion   **62**
The Large Magellanic Cloud   **64**
The Crab Nebula   **66**
Exoplanets   **68**

**What Is It Like For Humans
In Space?**   **70**
Earth's atmosphere   **72**
Astronomical observatories   **74**
Earth's artificial satellites   **76**
The space suit   **78**
Spacecraft   **80**
The International Space Station   **82**

Glossary   **84**

Index and Selected Sources   **86**

Look out for the galactic guide. It will be leading our intrepid explorers on an amazing tour of the universe. This three-eyed creature knows where to find all the best sights in the galaxy. It will act as teacher, pilot, spacecraft, and even space suit, to keep our explorers safe.

MAPPING THE STARS

Look up and admire the incredible spectacle that is space. It's amazing what you can see without even leaving the comfort of your own home! With approximately a billion trillion stars in the universe (and probably lots more!), what better place to begin our space journey?

CONSTELLATIONS
The night sky is a spectacular and vast place. Stars that shine in the blackness are many trillions of miles from Earth. People all around the world have connected the stars using imaginary lines, and given the shapes names. Often the names are based on myths and legends. These shapes are called constellations.

CELESTIAL EQUATOR

Cetus

Aquarius

Mira

Pegasus

Aries

Eridanus

Delphinus

Taurus

Triangulum

Aquila

Altair

Vulpecula
(Little Fox)

Cygnus

Cassiopeia

Algol

Pleiades

Hyades
Aldebaran

Rigel

Deneb

Perseus

Serpens
Cauda
(Serpent's
Tail)

Lyra

Vega

Cepheus

Ursa Minor
(Little Bear)

Polaris

Capella

Auriga

Orion

Betelgeuse

Hercules

Draco

Ursa Major
(Great Bear)

Ophiuchus

Corona
Borealis

Castor

Pollux

Gemini

Serpens
Caput
(Serpent's
Head)

Boötes

Lynx

Procyon

Canis Minor
(Lesser Dog)

Canes
Venatici
(Hunting
Dogs)

Arcturus

Libra

Regulus

Hydra

Leo

Virgo

Spica

THE SCIENTIFIC MAP OF THE SKY

In order to understand the night sky, ancient people imagined it reflected into a circular mirror. Today we still use this method and draw star maps in circles. On the left is the sky you see if you live in the northern half of the Earth. On the right is the sky that you see if you are in the south. The night sky looks different depending on where you see it from, on which day, and at what time. These maps show a sample of some of the best-known stars in the sky.

FINDING THE POLES
At the center of the map above is Polaris, which is also known as the North or Pole Star. It is a bright star that is nearest to the celestial pole. In the southern hemisphere, there is no single star that points south. However, there are some other stars that you can use to find your way: the Southern Cross and the Southern Pointers (Alpha and Beta Centauri).

6

The celestial equator is an imaginary line in the sky. It sits exactly opposite the equator—the imaginary line that runs around the center of the Earth.

CELESTIAL EQUATOR

Pegasus

Aquarius

Cetus

Mira

Taurus

Fomalhaut

Phoenix

Grus

Altair

Aquila

Eridanus

Achernar

Tucana

Capricornus

Serpens Cauda
(*Serpent's Tail*)

Orion

Rigel

Lepus

Dorado

Hydrus

Pavo

Sagittarius

Columba

Canopus

Volans

Apus

Ara

Scorpius

Serpens Caput
(*Serpent's Head*)

Betelgeuse

Musca

Triangulum Australe

Ophiuchus

Sirius

Carina

Alpha Centauri
Beta Centauri

Antares

Canis Major
(*Greater Dog*)

Puppis

Vela

Southern Cross

Lupus

Canis Minor
(*Lesser Dog*)

Centaurus

Libra

Procyon

Hydra

Corvus

Spica

MILKY WAY
The band that crosses these maps is the edge of the Milky Way, our galaxy.

Regulus

Virgo

7

Seasons in the northern hemisphere

Spring

Summer

Winter

Autumn

ROUND AND ROUND IT GOES

The Earth is not still, even though it might feel like it is. It spins on its axis (an imaginary rod through its center) and moves around the Sun at the same time. The spinning creates day and night, and makes it appear as though the Sun and the other stars are moving—just like when you are on a carousel and you look at the world around you. The movement around the Sun makes the seasons change. This is because the Earth is at an angle to the Sun, which changes where the Sun's rays fall on the planet. When the rays are direct, it is hotter; when they are on a slant, it is cooler.

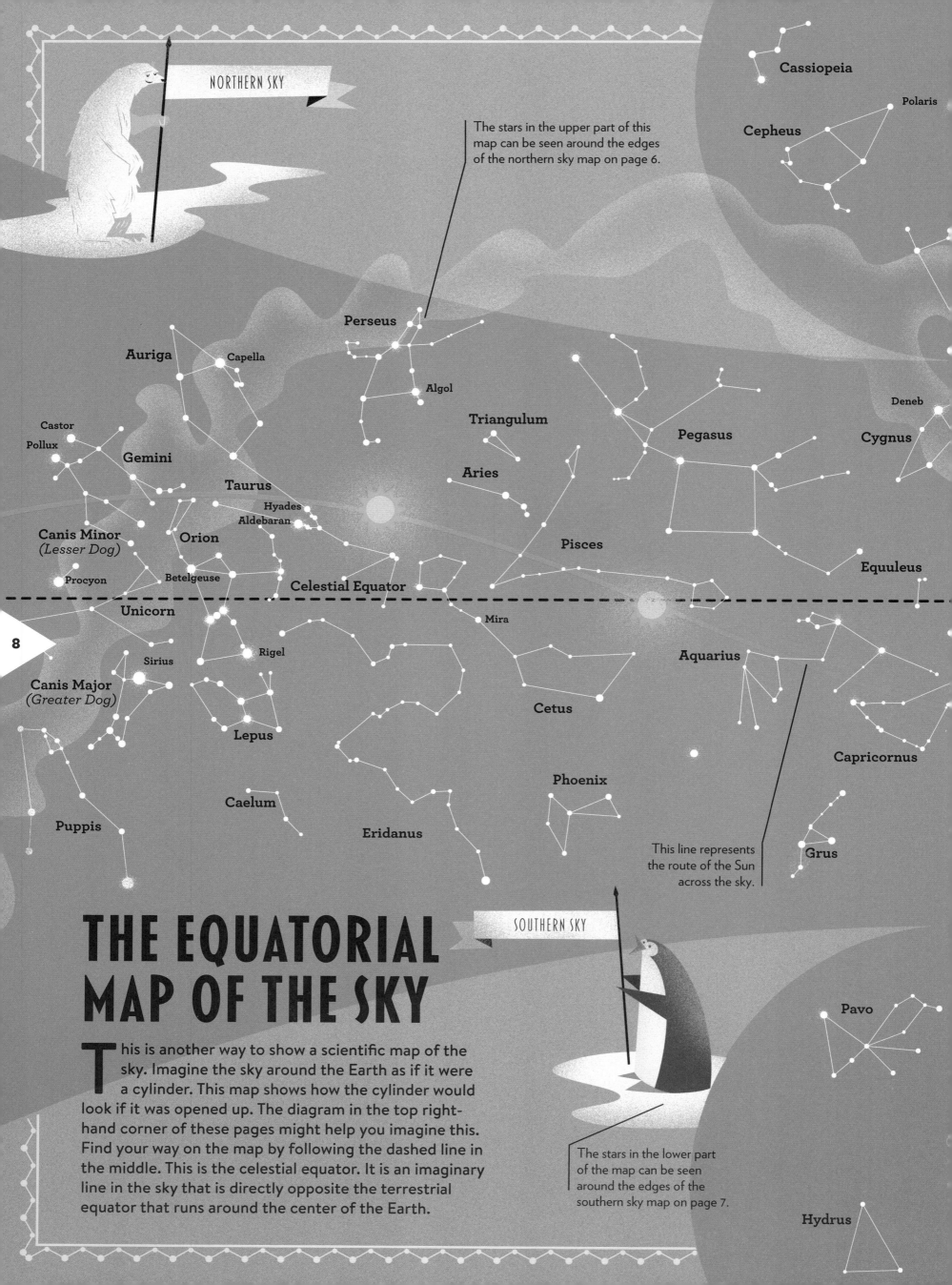

The stars in the upper part of this map can be seen around the edges of the northern sky map on page 6.

Cassiopeia

Polaris

Cepheus

Deneb

Perseus

Auriga

Capella

Algol

Triangulum

Pegasus

Cygnus

Aries

Gemini

Castor

Pollux

Taurus

Hyades

Aldebaran

Orion

Pisces

Canis Minor
(Lesser Dog)

Procyon

Betelgeuse

Celestial Equator

Equuleus

Unicorn

Mira

Aquarius

Sirius

Rigel

Canis Major
(Greater Dog)

Cetus

Capricornus

Lepus

Phoenix

Caelum

Grus

Puppis

Eridanus

This line represents the route of the Sun across the sky.

THE EQUATORIAL MAP OF THE SKY

This is another way to show a scientific map of the sky. Imagine the sky around the Earth as if it were a cylinder. This map shows how the cylinder would look if it was opened up. The diagram in the top right-hand corner of these pages might help you imagine this. Find your way on the map by following the dashed line in the middle. This is the celestial equator. It is an imaginary line in the sky that is directly opposite the terrestrial equator that runs around the center of the Earth.

Pavo

The stars in the lower part of the map can be seen around the edges of the southern sky map on page 7.

Hydrus

8

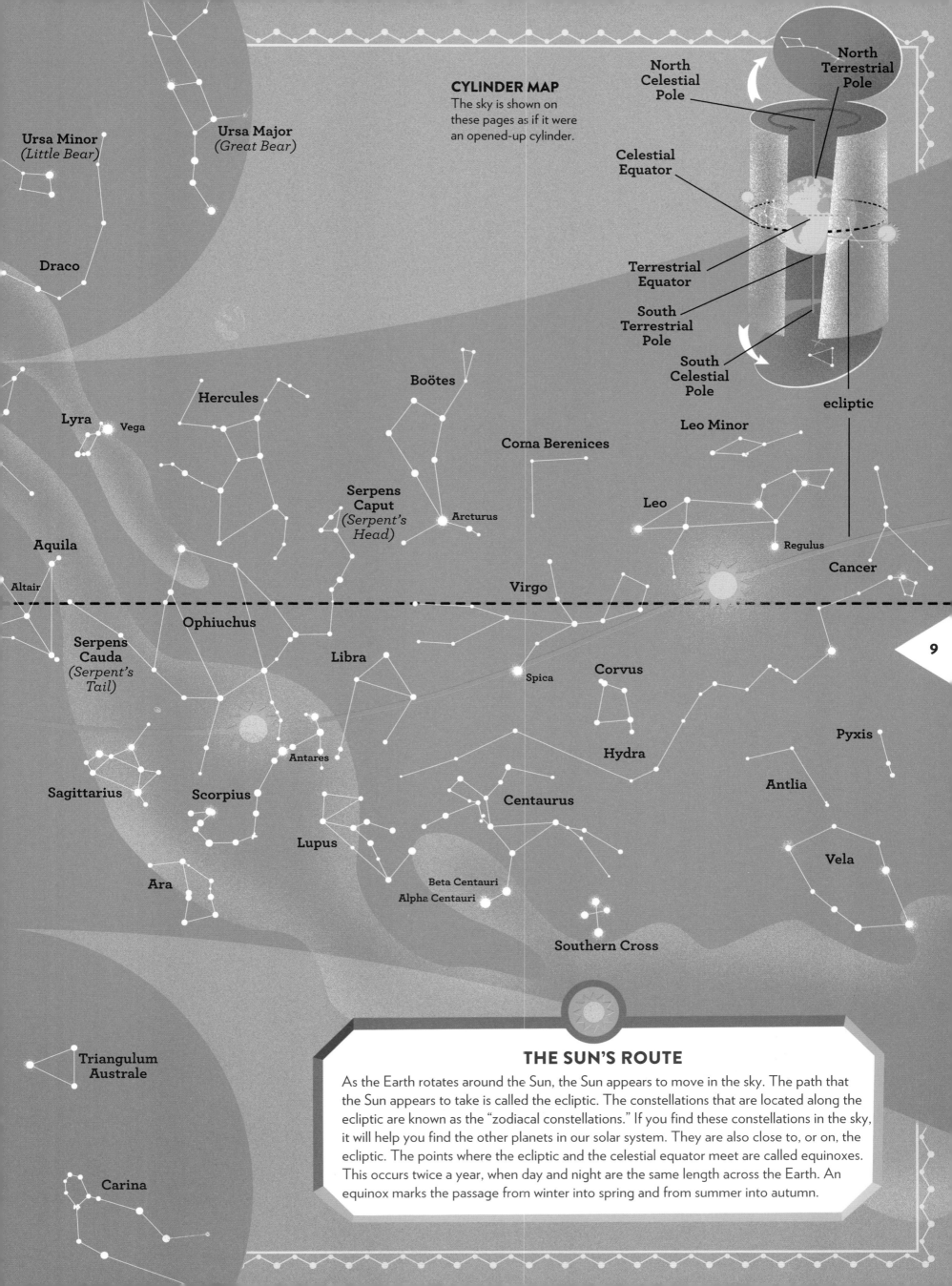

Ursa Minor
(Little Bear)

Ursa Major
(Great Bear)

Draco

CYLINDER MAP
The sky is shown on these pages as if it were an opened-up cylinder.

North Celestial Pole

North Terrestrial Pole

Celestial Equator

Terrestrial Equator

South Terrestrial Pole

South Celestial Pole

ecliptic

Boötes

Leo Minor

Lyra
Vega

Hercules

Corna Berenices

Serpens Caput
(Serpent's Head)

Leo

Aquila

Arcturus

Regulus

Cancer

Altair

Virgo

Ophiuchus

Serpens Cauda
(Serpent's Tail)

Libra

Spica

Corvus

Hydra

Pyxis

Antares

Antlia

Sagittarius

Scorpius

Centaurus

Vela

Lupus

Ara

Beta Centauri
Alpha Centauri

Southern Cross

Triangulum Australe

Carina

9

THE SUN'S ROUTE

As the Earth rotates around the Sun, the Sun appears to move in the sky. The path that the Sun appears to take is called the ecliptic. The constellations that are located along the ecliptic are known as the "zodiacal constellations." If you find these constellations in the sky, it will help you find the other planets in our solar system. They are also close to, or on, the ecliptic. The points where the ecliptic and the celestial equator meet are called equinoxes. This occurs twice a year, when day and night are the same length across the Earth. An equinox marks the passage from winter into spring and from summer into autumn.

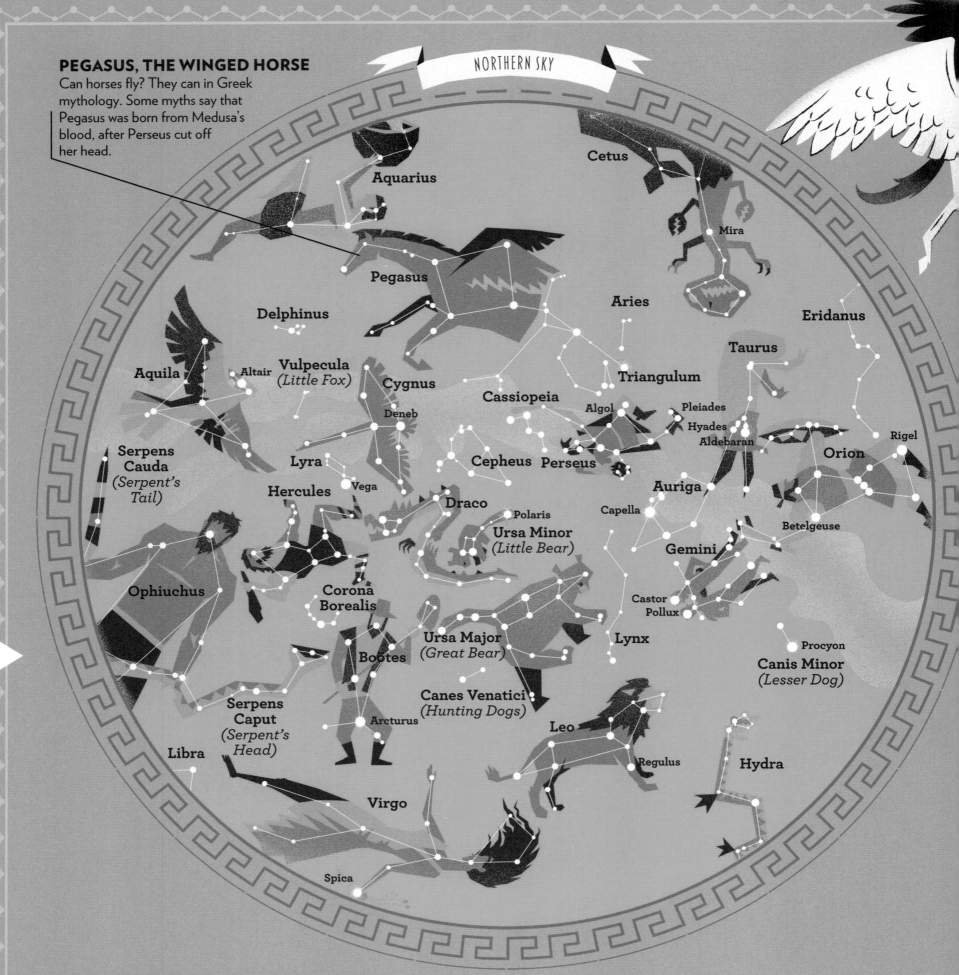

PEGASUS, THE WINGED HORSE
Can horses fly? They can in Greek mythology. Some myths say that Pegasus was born from Medusa's blood, after Perseus cut off her head.

Aquarius

Cetus

Mira

Pegasus

Aries

Eridanus

Delphinus

Taurus

Aquila

Altair

Vulpecula
(Little Fox)

Cygnus

Triangulum

Deneb

Cassiopeia

Algol

Pleiades
Hyades
Aldebaran

Rigel

Serpens
Cauda
*(Serpent's
Tail)*

Lyra

Cepheus

Perseus

Orion

Vega

Auriga

Capella

Betelgeuse

Hercules

Draco

Polaris

Ursa Minor
(Little Bear)

Gemini

Ophiuchus

Corona
Borealis

Castor
Pollux

Lynx

Ursa Major
(Great Bear)

Procyon

Boötes

Canis Minor
(Lesser Dog)

Serpens
Caput
*(Serpent's
Head)*

Arcturus

Canes Venatici
(Hunting Dogs)

Leo

Regulus

Hydra

Libra

Virgo

Spica

10

THE GREEK SKY

The ancient Greeks named the constellations that they saw in the sky after mythological figures. Among the stars they found Perseus, the son of the king, Zeus; Pegasus, the winged horse; the strong Hercules; and Medusa, who was able to turn people to stone with just one look. The International Astronomical Union decided to continue using these names, so many are still recognized today. They simply added other constellations that were not visible to the Greeks in order to complete the map, as shown here.

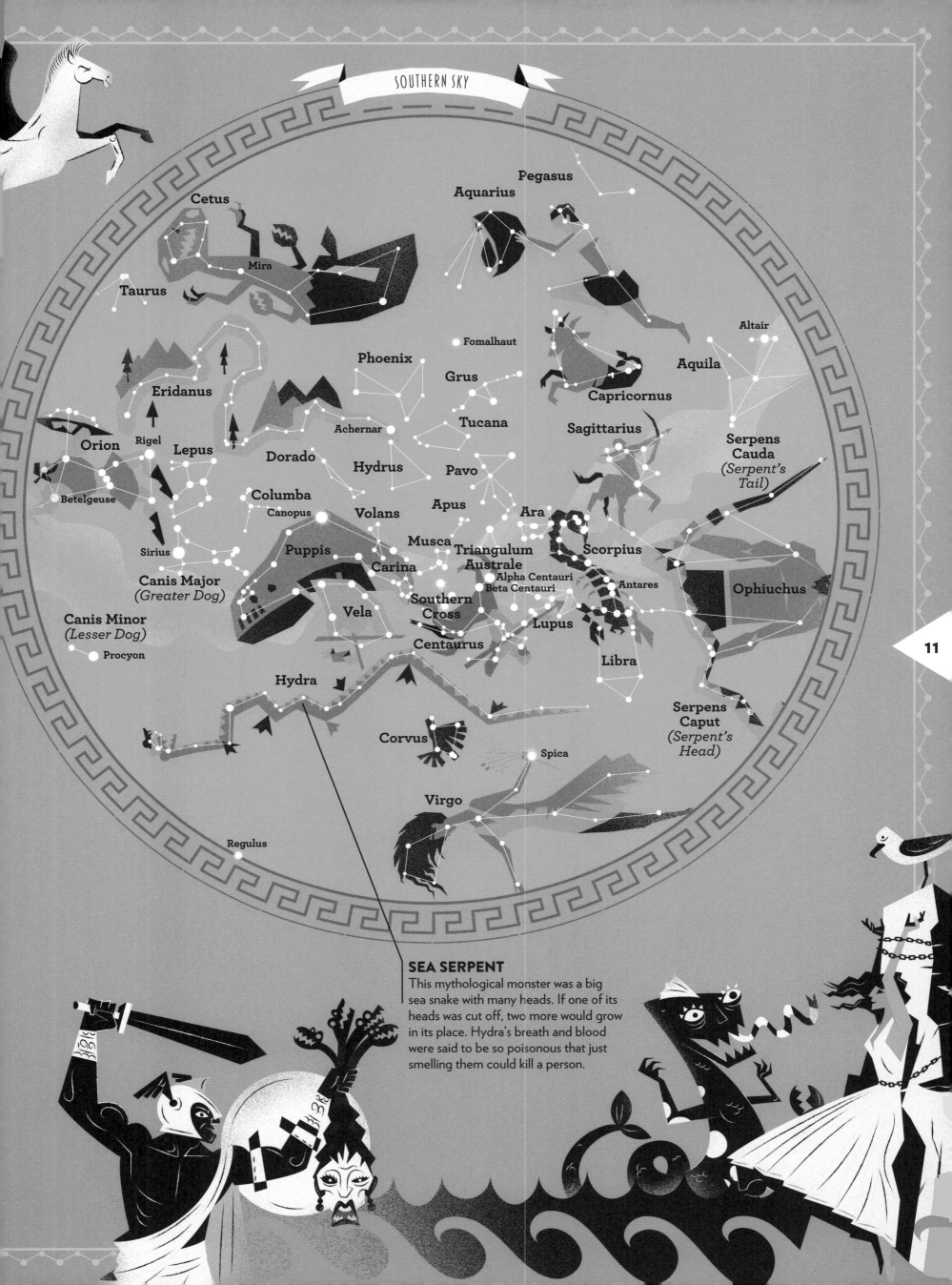

Cetus

Mira

Taurus

Pegasus

Aquarius

Fomalhaut

Phoenix

Grus

Altair

Aquila

Eridanus

Capricornus

Orion

Rigel

Lepus

Achernar

Tucana

Sagittarius

Serpens
Cauda
*(Serpent's
Tail)*

Betelgeuse

Dorado

Hydrus

Pavo

Columba

Canopus

Volans

Apus

Ara

Sirius

Musca

Triangulum
Australe

Scorpius

Ophiuchus

Canis Major
(Greater Dog)

Puppis

Carina

Alpha Centauri

Beta Centauri

Antares

Canis Minor
(Lesser Dog)

Vela

Southern
Cross

Lupus

Procyon

Centaurus

Libra

Hydra

Serpens
Caput
*(Serpent's
Head)*

Corvus

Spica

Virgo

Regulus

SEA SERPENT

This mythological monster was a big sea snake with many heads. If one of its heads was cut off, two more would grow in its place. Hydra's breath and blood were said to be so poisonous that just smelling them could kill a person.

11

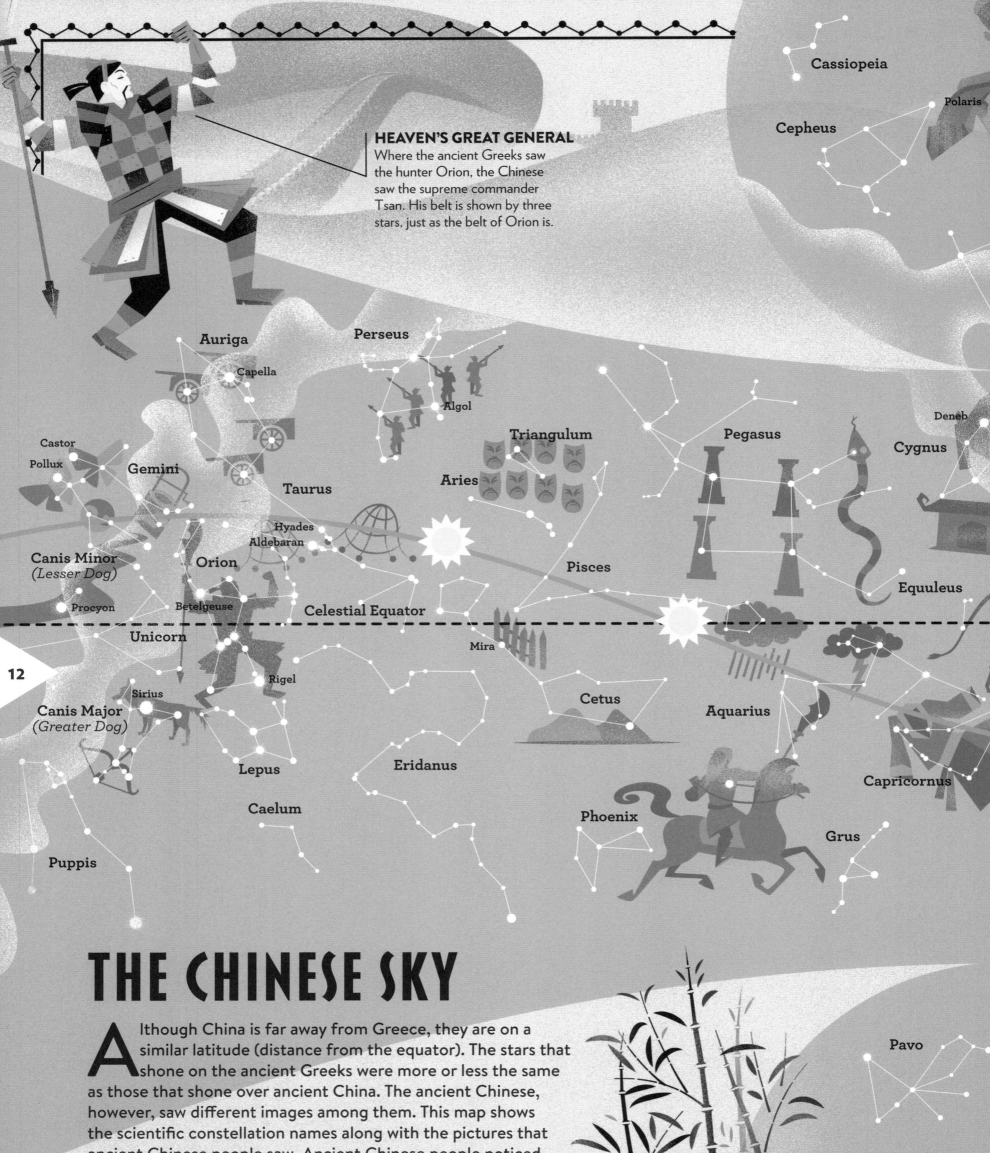

HEAVEN'S GREAT GENERAL
Where the ancient Greeks saw the hunter Orion, the Chinese saw the supreme commander Tsan. His belt is shown by three stars, just as the belt of Orion is.

Cassiopeia

Polaris

Cepheus

Auriga

Perseus

Capella

Algol

Deneb

Triangulum

Pegasus

Cygnus

Castor

Pollux

Gemini

Aries

Taurus

Hyades

Aldebaran

Canis Minor
(*Lesser Dog*)

Orion

Pisces

Procyon

Betelgeuse

Equuleus

Unicorn

Celestial Equator

Mira

Rigel

Cetus

Aquarius

Canis Major
(*Greater Dog*)

Sirius

Lepus

Eridanus

Capricornus

Caelum

Phoenix

Grus

Puppis

Pavo

THE CHINESE SKY

Although China is far away from Greece, they are on a similar latitude (distance from the equator). The stars that shone on the ancient Greeks were more or less the same as those that shone over ancient China. The ancient Chinese, however, saw different images among them. This map shows the scientific constellation names along with the pictures that ancient Chinese people saw. Ancient Chinese people noticed that all the stars in the sky appear to move around Polaris. So it became the center of one of their legends. This legend said that there were four heavenly ministers who were in charge of heaven and Earth. One of these ministers was called the Emperor, and he could be found with Polaris, in the center of the sky.

Hydrus

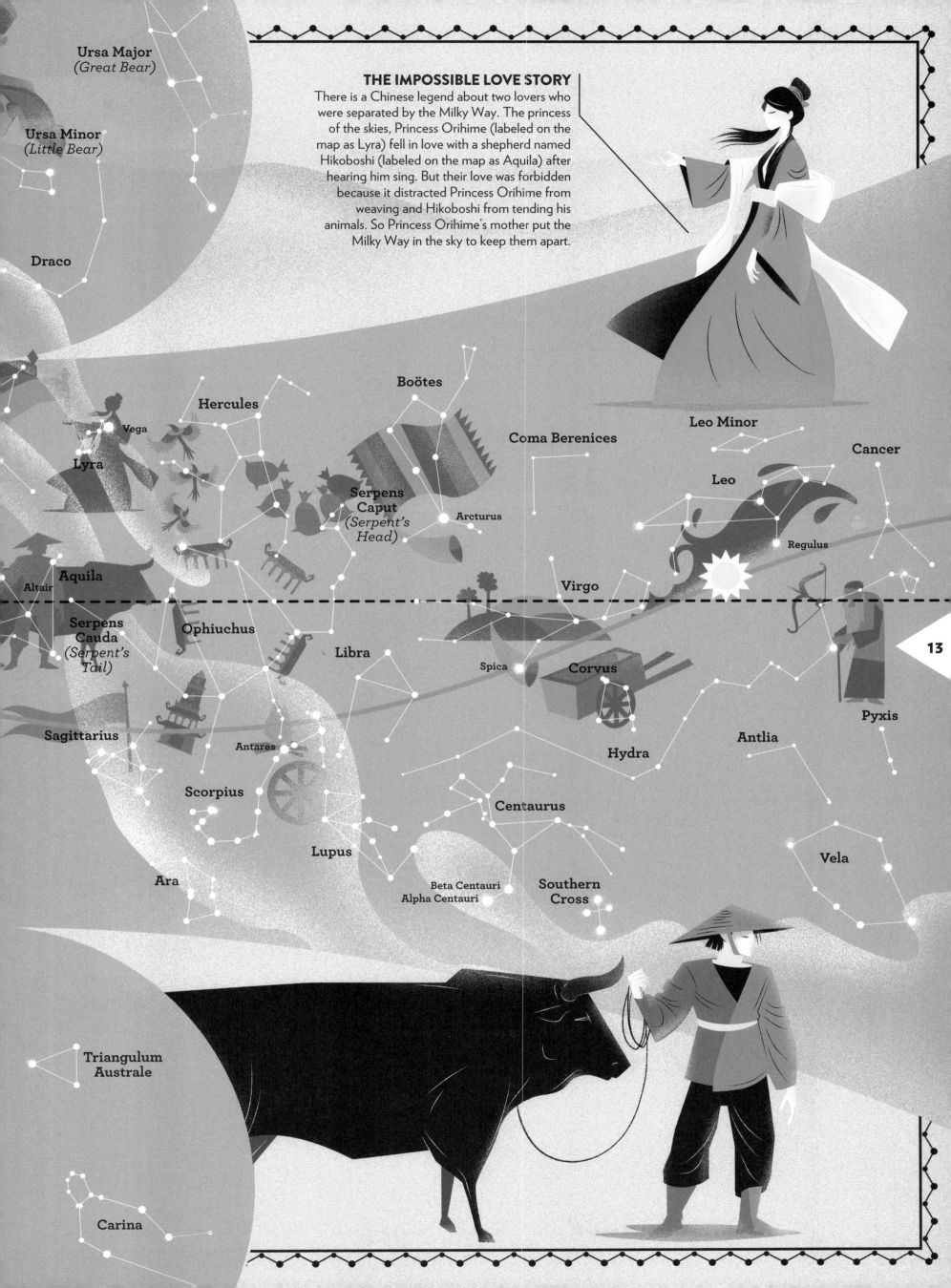

Ursa Major
(Great Bear)

Ursa Minor
(Little Bear)

Draco

THE IMPOSSIBLE LOVE STORY
There is a Chinese legend about two lovers who were separated by the Milky Way. The princess of the skies, Princess Orihime (labeled on the map as Lyra) fell in love with a shepherd named Hikoboshi (labeled on the map as Aquila) after hearing him sing. But their love was forbidden because it distracted Princess Orihime from weaving and Hikoboshi from tending his animals. So Princess Orihime's mother put the Milky Way in the sky to keep them apart.

Hercules

Boötes

Vega

Lyra

Serpens Caput
(Serpent's Head)

Arcturus

Coma Berenices

Leo Minor

Cancer

Leo

Regulus

Altair

Aquila

Virgo

Serpens Cauda
(Serpent's Tail)

Ophiuchus

Libra

Spica

Corvus

Sagittarius

Antares

Hydra

Antlia

Pyxis

Scorpius

Centaurus

Lupus

Southern Cross

Vela

Ara

Beta Centauri
Alpha Centauri

Triangulum Australe

Carina

THE SOUTH AFRICAN SKY

Africa is such a large continent that it crosses the equator. For this reason, the celestial landscape changes a lot depending on where it is viewed from. This map shows a part of the sky as it would look from South Africa. It includes the scientific constellation names along with the pictures that the San people of southern Africa saw. The San understood and named these pictures based on their culture and traditions. Many of them take the form of animals such as zebras, giraffes, and lions. The San people also saw the eyes of wild animals in some of the brightest stars in the sky.

GOD IN THE SKY

One San story tells of three zebras that escaped capture by running so fast that they ran up into the sky. They became the three stars in Orion's belt. Another story is about the Pleiades, a star cluster near the Taurus constellation, shown on the northern sky maps. These stars were the daughters of the sky god. One day their husband, Aldebaran, went hunting and tried to shoot the zebras. However, he missed and the arrow landed near a fierce lion, which is what the San saw Betelgeuse as. Aldebaran couldn't return home without food and it was too dangerous to collect his arrow, so he sat alone in the dark. He is still there to this day.

THE LOST ROAD

There was once a man who became lost in the wilderness and surrounded by fierce wild beasts. To show him the way home, his wife threw the embers of a fire up into the sky. The shining embers created the Milky Way, and many people now call it "the road of stars."

Pegasus

Aquarius

Taurus

Cetus

Mira

Capricornus

Altair

Eridanus

Phoenix

Fomalhaut

Grus

Aquila

Achernar

Tucana

Sagittarius

Orion

Rigel

Lepus

Dorado

Hydrus

Pavo

Serpens
Cauda
*(Serpent's
Tail)*

Columba

Betelgeuse

Canopus

Volans

Apus

Ara

Canis
Major
*(Greater
Dog)*

Sirius

Musca

Triangulum
Australe

Scorpius

Ophiuchus

Carina

Alpha Centauri

Antares

Beta Centauri

Canis Minor
(Lesser Dog)

Puppis

Vela

Southern Cross

Lupus

Procyon

Centaurus

Libra

Hydra

Serpens
Caput
*(Serpent's
Head)*

Corvus

Spica

Virgo

Regulus

15

GRANDMOTHER IN
THE STARS
Canopus is a yellow-white
supergiant star located around
310 light-years from Earth. San
people referred to it as "Granny
Canopus." Granny's stomach was
said to be full of food and light.
The San prayed to her when they
were hungry or needed light.

SPACE FIRE
Antares, the red star in the
Scorpius constellation, was
known as the "fire-finishing star."
It appeared late at night, when
the fires were dying down and
all that was left were red embers.

Our extraterrestrial escort is going to be our heroes' spaceship and space suit. It will keep them safe once they leave planet Earth. Hold on to your helmets as we journey through the solar system!

WHERE ARE WE?

The Sun is at the center of our solar system, and our solar system is in the Milky Way galaxy. The Milky Way is in the universe, which is so vast that we don't even know how big it is! In order to try to understand the universe, humans have studied it with probes and telescopes, and they have found some fascinating things. However, there is still plenty more to discover...

GALAXIES

The dots and swirls that you see on this map are galaxies. It is thought that there could be as many as 100 billion galaxies in the universe. When viewed through a powerful telescope, the shape of some galaxies can be seen. However, many others are so far away that their form is not clear.

A MILLION LIGHT-YEARS

LIGHT-YEARS
Distances in space are so big that they can't be measured in the same way as on Earth. Otherwise the numbers would become mind-bogglingly huge. So instead, distances in space are measured in light-years. In one year, light can travel approximately 6 trillion miles (9 trillion km) —that's one light-year. The square image above represents an area of the sky that is one million light-years across, which is a really massive distance.

SPIRAL GALAXY COLORS
Spiral-shaped galaxies come in many exciting colors. The center is usually yellow-red, which means that it contains older stars that have cooled down. The arms of the spiral are usually bluish and include young or newborn stars.

BLUE GALAXIES
Blue galaxies often include lots of young and extremely hot stars. When captured on camera, their images can appear red. This happens because their light changes as it travels through space.

BARRED SPIRAL GALAXIES
Barred spiral galaxies have two arms branching off the ends of a bar-shaped structure that runs through their middle.

SPIRAL GALAXIES
These galaxies are composed of a central core surrounded by a disc of stars. This disc separates into long, curved "arms."

6
5
4
3
2
1

WHAT IS GRAVITY?

Gravity is one of the most important things in the universe—without it, nothing would stay in place. It is a force that pulls objects together, and the strength of it depends on the mass of the objects. Mass is calculated by the amount of matter, or physical substance, an object has. Earth's gravity is quite strong, because it is a planet with a large mass. This means that everything on Earth, including you, is pulled toward its center. The Moon's gravity, on the other hand, is much weaker. So if you were to jump upward on the Moon, it would take much longer for you to be pulled back down. In space, all bodies (such as planets and moons) are pulled toward one another by gravity. This is what keeps planets in orbit around the Sun.

THE MILKY WAY

This is what we think our galaxy would look like if it were seen from the top. We are inside the galaxy looking out, so gaining this overview is not easy. Space travel is not yet advanced enough for a craft to travel outside of the Milky Way and take a photograph of it. However, by studying the stars, scientists have been able to gather evidence that allows them to figure out what shape the Milky Way is—it is a spiral. They also have an idea of what else is inside it.

Scutum-Centaurus Arm

Norma Arm

Sagittarius Arm

Galaxy core

26,000 LIGHT-YEARS

Orion Spur

Perseus Arm

ARMS

Scientists have been able to find four arms (regions of stars) in our galaxy. It is thought that there are two main arms called Scutum-Centaurus and Perseus. Then there are also two thinner arms called the Norma Arm and the Sagittarius Arm. All of the arms spiral out of the central core. Our Sun is located in a small, partial arm called the Orion Spur.

THE SUN

Here is our Sun: it is approximately 26,000 light-years from the galaxy core.

This is what the Milky Way would look like from the side.

STELLAR NURSERIES

This red-orange area is a stellar nursery. Here, the new stars of our galaxy are being continuously born.

SAGITTARIUS A*

This supermassive black hole is at the center of our galaxy. Its mass is about four million times that of our Sun, and it is 26,000 light-years away from Earth.

100,000 LIGHT-YEARS

HOW BIG IS OUR GALAXY?

Light takes 100,000 light-years to cross the Milky Way from one side to the other, so our galaxy has a diameter of approximately 100,000 light-years.

In 2019, scientists took the first picture of a black hole's silhouette. They used a network of super-strong telescopes called the Event Horizon Telescope.

BLACK HOLE: SPACE'S DEEP DARKNESS

Black holes are strange things. They are places where the force of gravity is so strong that nothing can escape, not even light. They are actually invisible, and we only know that they are there because of how they affect the things around them. A black hole is a bit like a vacuum cleaner; if an object moves close to it, it is sucked in by gravity and disappears. There could be millions of black holes in the Milky Way. There are three different types: the smallest are stellar black holes, formed when a star explodes and collapses in on itself. Intermediate mass black holes are medium-sized, and supermassive black holes are the largest.

THE SUN

The Sun is a star like many others, but it is very special to us. It is located 93 million miles (150 million km) from the Earth and gives us light and heat. The Sun is essentially a gigantic ball of fire. It is made of a collection of very hot gases that are held together by gravity. The Sun's core acts as a large nuclear power plant, making the star extremely hot. The core produces vast amounts of energy that it pushes up to the boiling surface. In comparison to other stars, our Sun is medium-sized and middle-aged. It is about halfway through its lifespan.

PHOTOSPHERE

This is the surface of the Sun, the part of the star that we can see from the Earth. It is transparent and has a granular structure, which means it is not smooth. The Sun is made of gas, so its surface is not solid. The temperature here is around 10,000°F (5,500°C).

CHROMOSPHERE

This is the atmosphere above the photosphere. It can reach temperatures of 36,000°F (20,000°C).

CORONA

This is the outer layer of the Sun's atmosphere. It stretches for millions of miles and its high temperature causes gases to shoot out into space. These fast-moving gases are called solar wind and can reach speeds of 500 miles (800 km) per second.

SUNSPOTS

These dark spots are caused when an area is cooler than the rest of the Sun's surface. Each spot is very large, and many have a surface area that is bigger than that of the Earth! They have short lifespans and often disappear after just a few weeks.

Size of Earth for comparison

SOLAR FLARES

Sometimes there will be sudden flashes of brightness in the photosphere. These are called solar flares and often occur near sunspots. They are violent explosions that give out enormous amounts of energy.

THE SUN

MASS	333,000 times that of the Earth
DIAMETER	865,000 miles (1,392,000 km)—that is 109 times the diameter of the Earth
TEMPERATURE ON THE SURFACE	10,000°F (5,500°C)
TEMPERATURE AT THE CENTER	27 million°F (15 million°C)
COMPOSITION	70% hydrogen, 28% helium, 2% other elements

IDENTITY CARD

CORE

This is the center of the Sun, the place where all the Sun's energy is produced. Inside it, where the temperature reaches 27 million degrees Fahrenheit (15 million degrees Celsius), hydrogen is transformed into helium. This process is called nuclear fusion and creates a lot of energy. The energy travels through the Sun until it reaches the surface. There, it makes the surface of the Sun incredibly hot and bright.

SOLAR PROMINENCES

These are gas clouds that start from the photosphere and stretch into the corona. They often form in loops and can reach heights of 500,000 miles (800,000 km).

THE LIFE OF THE SUN

Let's make a run for it!

3. A red giant

1. A young blue star

2. A yellow star

4. A white dwarf

WILL THE SUN LIVE FOREVER?

The Sun is yellow, like all middle-aged stars. As it ages, it will cool, change color to red, and grow to an enormous size. When the Sun expands, it is thought that all life on Earth will end. Don't let that scare you, though; this won't happen for at least another four and a half billion years. By then, humans may have escaped to a distant planet! Finally, the Sun will collapse, shrink, and become a white dwarf.

THE SOLAR SYSTEM

The Earth is not the Sun's only satellite. Many other planets and celestial bodies also orbit this star. In total there are eight planets in our solar system: Mercury, Venus, Earth, Mars, Jupiter, Saturn, Uranus, and Neptune. There are also several dwarf planets, many moons, asteroids, and comets, and an awful lot of dust.

THE PLANETS' ORBITS
The path that a planet takes around the Sun is called an orbit. Planets are kept on these paths by a specific, and delicate, balance of forces. When something moves, it will go in a straight line unless something pushes or pulls it—this is called momentum. Planets are kept in orbit around the Sun because their momentum is balanced with the Sun's gravity.

Sun

Jupiter

Venus

Moon

Mercury

Earth

Mars

THE EARTH'S AVERAGE ORBITAL SPEED
This is the speed at which the Earth moves around the Sun. It is approximately 19 miles (30 km) per second.

ASTEROID BELT
In between Mars and Jupiter, there is an area that is full of thousands of rocky objects. The objects are called asteroids. They move in elliptical (oval-shaped) orbits around the Sun. However, the force of a nearby planet's gravity can pull one off course. This can cause the asteroid to crash into the surface of a planet or moon somewhere else in the solar system. The impact of this collision can form a crater.

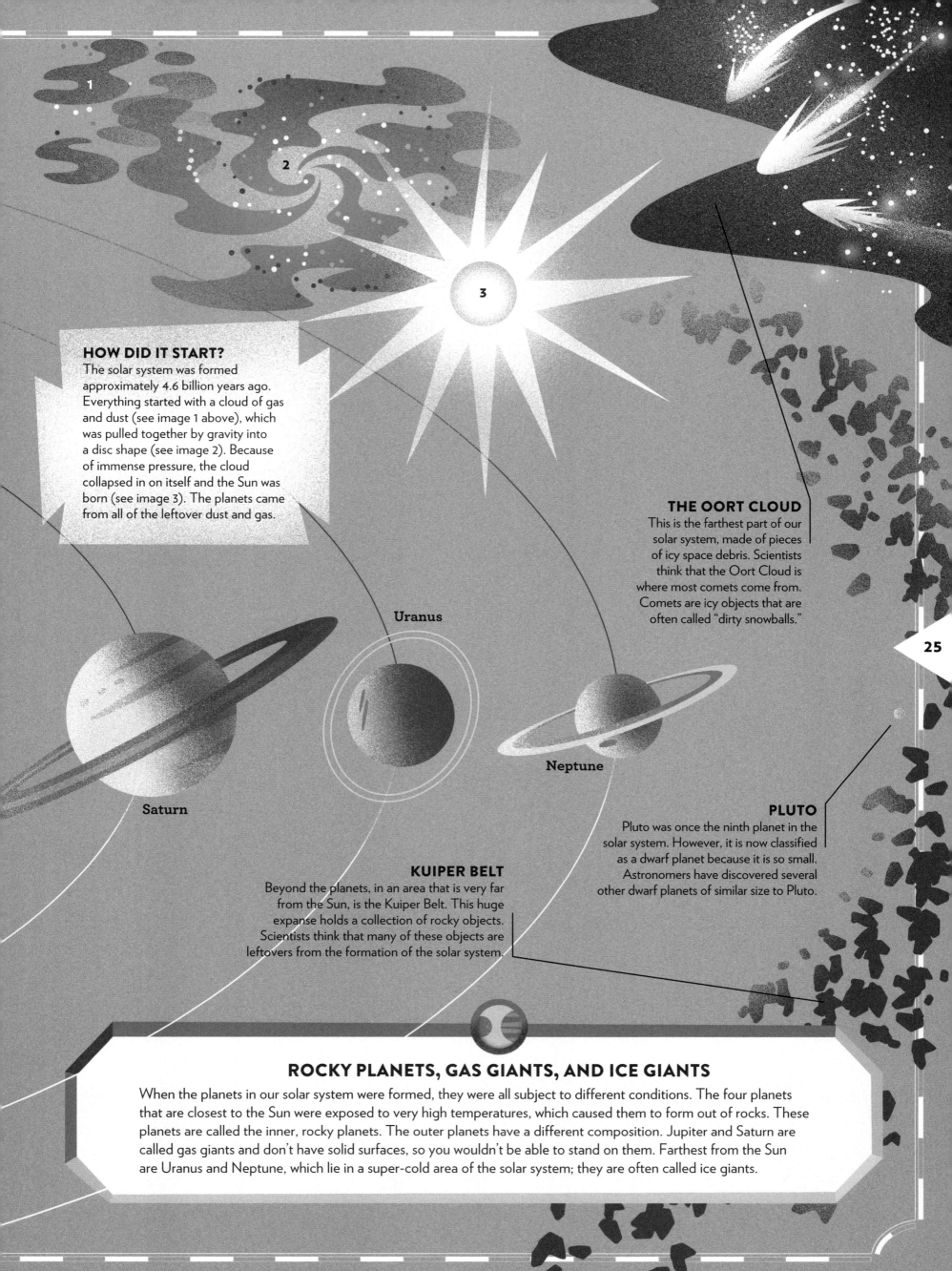

1

2

3

HOW DID IT START?

The solar system was formed approximately 4.6 billion years ago. Everything started with a cloud of gas and dust (see image 1 above), which was pulled together by gravity into a disc shape (see image 2). Because of immense pressure, the cloud collapsed in on itself and the Sun was born (see image 3). The planets came from all of the leftover dust and gas.

THE OORT CLOUD

This is the farthest part of our solar system, made of pieces of icy space debris. Scientists think that the Oort Cloud is where most comets come from. Comets are icy objects that are often called "dirty snowballs."

Uranus

Neptune

Saturn

PLUTO

Pluto was once the ninth planet in the solar system. However, it is now classified as a dwarf planet because it is so small. Astronomers have discovered several other dwarf planets of similar size to Pluto.

KUIPER BELT

Beyond the planets, in an area that is very far from the Sun, is the Kuiper Belt. This huge expanse holds a collection of rocky objects. Scientists think that many of these objects are leftovers from the formation of the solar system.

ROCKY PLANETS, GAS GIANTS, AND ICE GIANTS

When the planets in our solar system were formed, they were all subject to different conditions. The four planets that are closest to the Sun were exposed to very high temperatures, which caused them to form out of rocks. These planets are called the inner, rocky planets. The outer planets have a different composition. Jupiter and Saturn are called gas giants and don't have solid surfaces, so you wouldn't be able to stand on them. Farthest from the Sun are Uranus and Neptune, which lie in a super-cold area of the solar system; they are often called ice giants.

JOURNEYS THROUGH THE SOLAR SYSTEM

Humans have not yet traveled farther than the far side of the Moon. But we have launched probes to explore for us. Many of them have used the "gravity assist" technique to gain speed and travel as far as possible. To do this, the probe goes into orbit around the Earth, which causes it to pick up speed. It then performs a slingshot maneuver to propel it out into the solar system. Here are just a few of the amazing missions that have been sent to discover what is in our solar system.

MESSENGER (USA)

In 2004 the Messenger probe was launched to explore Mercury. It stayed in orbit around the planet for just over four years. The probe discovered what Mercury is made of, how its magnetic field works, and also found water-ice at its poles. The mission ended in a spectacular fashion when the probe smashed into Mercury's surface.

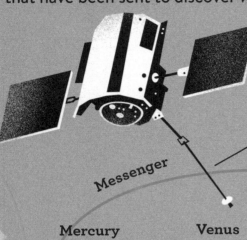

Sun

Mercury

Venus

Messenger

Moon

Earth

Lunar missions

Mars missions

Mars

Jupiter

Venera 7

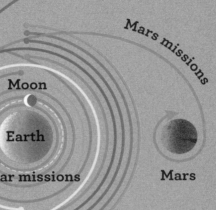

SOHO

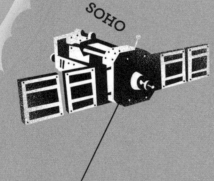
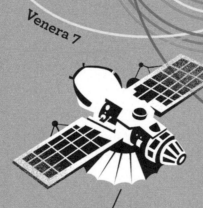

Galileo

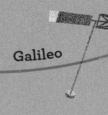

SOHO (USA AND EUROPE)

Launched in 1995, SOHO has given us lots of information about the Sun and surrounding comets. It is still working today and is very smart. SOHO has 12 different scientific instruments on board that observe many aspects of the Sun at the same time.

VENERA 7 (RUSSIA)

In 1970, this was the first probe to land on Venus. It was the first human-made object to land on another planet and transmit data back to the Earth.

SPUTNIK 1 (RUSSIA)

In 1957, this Russian probe was the first human-made object to be launched into space. It went into orbit around the Earth and sent back information about the atmosphere.

VOSTOK 1 (RUSSIA)

"The Earth is blue. How wonderful. It is so beautiful!" This is what Yuri Gagarin said in 1961, when he went on the first journey into space aboard Vostok 1. While walking toward the launch pad, Gagarin stopped to pee on the rear wheel of the bus that had taken him there. It is now a good luck tradition for Russian cosmonauts to do the same before they blast off.

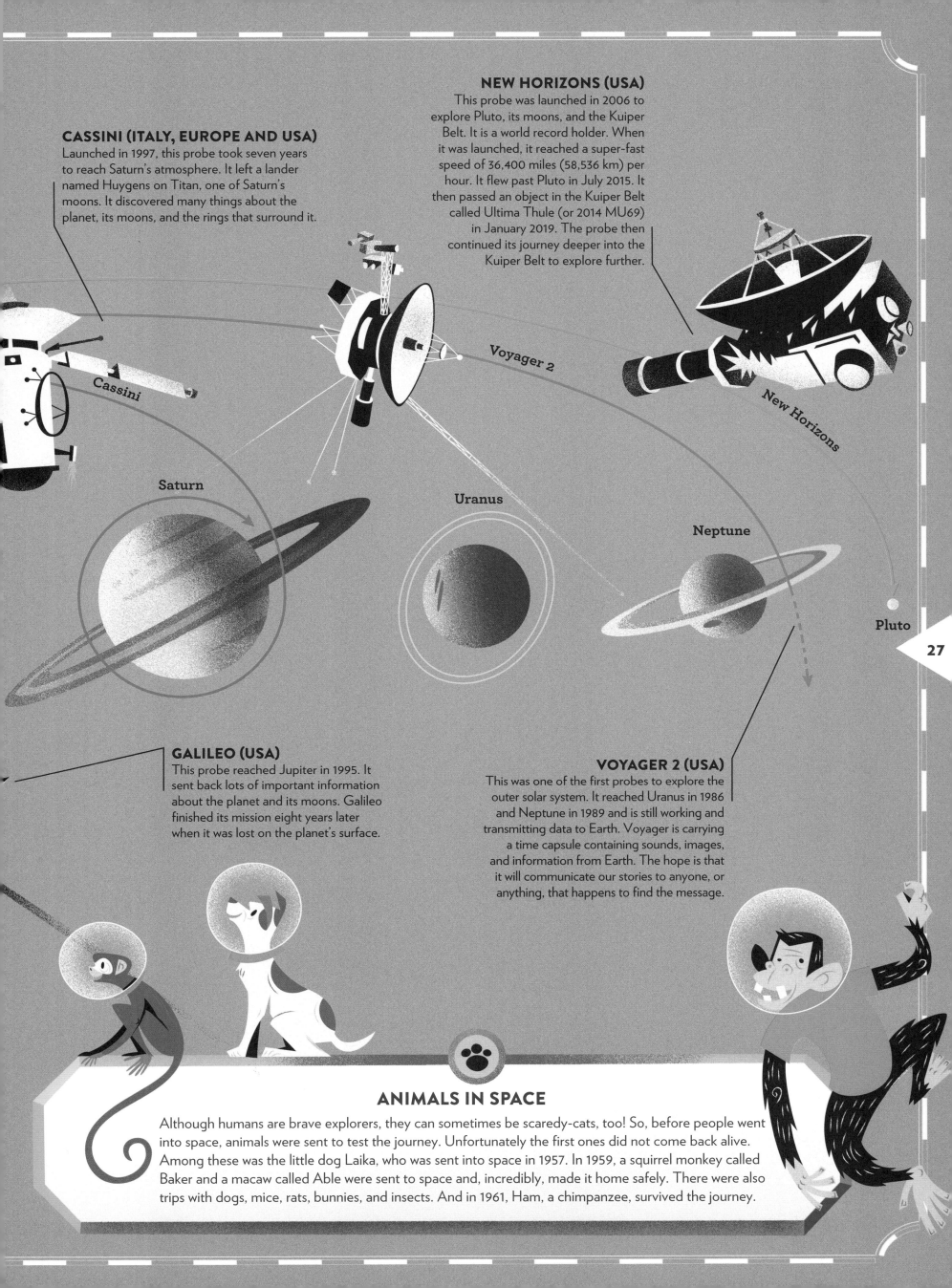

CASSINI (ITALY, EUROPE AND USA)

Launched in 1997, this probe took seven years to reach Saturn's atmosphere. It left a lander named Huygens on Titan, one of Saturn's moons. It discovered many things about the planet, its moons, and the rings that surround it.

NEW HORIZONS (USA)

This probe was launched in 2006 to explore Pluto, its moons, and the Kuiper Belt. It is a world record holder. When it was launched, it reached a super-fast speed of 36,400 miles (58,536 km) per hour. It flew past Pluto in July 2015. It then passed an object in the Kuiper Belt called Ultima Thule (or 2014 MU69) in January 2019. The probe then continued its journey deeper into the Kuiper Belt to explore further.

Cassini

Voyager 2

New Horizons

Saturn

Uranus

Neptune

Pluto

GALILEO (USA)

This probe reached Jupiter in 1995. It sent back lots of important information about the planet and its moons. Galileo finished its mission eight years later when it was lost on the planet's surface.

VOYAGER 2 (USA)

This was one of the first probes to explore the outer solar system. It reached Uranus in 1986 and Neptune in 1989 and is still working and transmitting data to Earth. Voyager is carrying a time capsule containing sounds, images, and information from Earth. The hope is that it will communicate our stories to anyone, or anything, that happens to find the message.

ANIMALS IN SPACE

Although humans are brave explorers, they can sometimes be scaredy-cats, too! So, before people went into space, animals were sent to test the journey. Unfortunately the first ones did not come back alive. Among these was the little dog Laika, who was sent into space in 1957. In 1959, a squirrel monkey called Baker and a macaw called Able were sent to space and, incredibly, made it home safely. There were also trips with dogs, mice, rats, bunnies, and insects. And in 1961, Ham, a chimpanzee, survived the journey.

THE EARTH'S DIAMETER
Imagine a straight line going through the Earth, from the north pole to the south pole. This is how we measure the diameter of a planet. The diameter of the Earth measures 7,900 miles (12,714 km). At the poles there are ice caps, and at the core there is a solid ball of metal, surrounded by molten magma.

DESERTS
These are areas with very little water, where only a few animals and plants can survive. Technically, Antarctica is the largest desert on Earth. However, the Sahara Desert, in Africa, is the largest non-polar desert in the world. The Atacama Desert, in Chile, is the driest.

Arctic Ocean

NORTH AMERICA

EUROPE

Atlantic Ocean

Earth's diameter

Sahara Desert

AFRICA

Pacific Ocean

Amazon River

SOUTH AMERICA

Atacama Desert

THE CRUST
The large areas of land on Earth are called continents. They are on the Earth's crust, which is the outermost layer of the planet. The crust is a jigsaw of giant pieces called tectonic plates. The slow movement of the pieces can cause earthquakes and volcanic eruptions.

WATERY PLANET
Water covers 71% of Earth. The oceans hold 96.5% of it as salt water. Then 1.7% is stored as ice and 1.7% is fresh water in rivers, lakes, groundwater, and the atmosphere. The total amount is 333 million cubic miles (1.388 billion cubic km). The deepest place on Earth is the Mariana Trench at more than 36,000 feet (11,000 m) deep, and the longest river is the Amazon at 4,345 miles (6,992 km).

THE EARTH

Planet Earth sits in the Goldilocks Zone of the solar system. This is the only area that we know of that has the right conditions to support life. It is not too hot and not too cold. Because the temperature is just right, there is liquid water for creatures to drink. There is also an atmosphere, which means that there is air to breathe. The numerous and immense oceans give our planet its characteristic blue color. When it is observed from space, it looks like a huge blue marble.

IDENTITY CARD

EARTH

TYPE OF PLANET	Rocky
DISTANCE FROM THE SUN	3rd planet from the Sun— 93 million miles (149.6 million km)
DIAMETER	7,900 miles (12,714 km)
TIME OF REVOLUTION	365 days
TIME OF ROTATION	24 hours
MOONS	1 (The Moon)

ROTATION AXIS

The Earth rotates once a day, from west to east, around an imaginary axis that goes from the north to the south pole.

MOUNTAINS

The highest mountain in the world is Everest. It is part of the Himalayan mountain range and sits on the border between Nepal and China. Mount Everest rises an astonishing 29,029 feet (8,848 m) above sea level.

ASIA

AFRICA

Mount Everest

Indian Ocean

Pacific Ocean

Mariana Trench

Mauna Loa volcano

AUSTRALIA

VOLCANOES

When a volcano erupts, lava, ash, and rock fragments are thrown high up into the air. This material comes from inside the Earth. It is forced up by heat and pressure, which builds up under the crust. Mauna Loa in Hawaii is the biggest volcano in the world.

Antarctic Ocean

SOLAR ECLIPSE

A solar eclipse happens when the Moon passes between the Earth and the Sun. When the three celestial bodies are perfectly aligned, the Moon completely blocks the Sun's rays, plunging the Earth into darkness. We call this a total eclipse. If the Sun is only partially blocked, then we call it a partial eclipse; and if only a thin bright ring of the Sun is visible, we call it an annular eclipse.

WESTERN EUROPE AND NORTH AMERICA
Here light pollution is very common. Some studies have suggested that 99% of people living in these areas rarely experience a natural night.

AFRICA AND SOUTH AMERICA
In these areas of the Earth, the sky is still quite dark. Both continents are in the southern hemisphere, which is less affected by light pollution because fewer people live there.

DESERTS
Deserts are the darkest places on the Earth because fewer people live there. Astronomers have placed many telescopes in the Atacama Desert in Chile. Stars can be seen very well from there.

LIGHT POLLUTION

If you were to look down on Earth from space during nighttime, you would see it covered in millions of tiny lights. These are the artificial lights that humans use to see in the dark. Each one is a street lamp, car headlight, shop sign, or light from our homes. The brightest lights are concentrated in areas that are more built up, where lots of people live. Unfortunately, artificial lights cause light pollution. They make it difficult to see stars, planets, or the edge of the Milky Way in the night sky. The light patches on this map show the places that are most affected by light pollution around the world.

WHAT IS LIGHT POLLUTION?
Light pollution is when artificial lights are used so much that they outshine any light coming from the Moon or stars. This means that stars cannot be seen in the night sky. Light pollution is bad for the sleep patterns of both humans and animals. It is also bad for the environment, as electric lights use up our valuable energy resources.

SOUTH KOREA
South Korea is one of the countries with the worst light pollution. The country has now set up a committee to police artificial light levels in certain areas.

HONG KONG
This city is known for its many bright neon buildings. The light pollution here is so bad that on average the night sky is hundreds of times brighter than a natural night sky.

SAUDI ARABIA
It is almost impossible for most people who live here to see the Milky Way.

SINGAPORE
There is maximum light pollution here.

AUSTRALIA
Australia is one of the darkest continents. It is so dark because of its vast spaces and scarce population.

OBSERVING THE MILKY WAY
The edge of the Milky Way, the beautiful cloudy band that crosses our night skies, cannot be seen when there are high levels of light pollution. For this reason it is used to measure light pollution in the sky in different places on the Earth. Can you see the Milky Way from your home?

SEA OF SHOWERS
It is possible to spot this area from Earth, without using a telescope. Because of this, there are many stories about the characters that people have imagined living there.

LUNAR APENNINES
This is the most impressive mountain range on the Moon. It extends for approximately 370 miles (600 km). Some of its peaks are higher than 13,000 feet (4,000 m). That's a similar height to the Mauna Kea volcano in Hawaii.

COPERNICUS CRATER
This crater has a diameter of 58 miles (93 km). It is very deep; on average, it reaches a depth of 12,300 feet (3,760 m). It was probably formed by an asteroid or comet that crashed into the Moon's surface.

Lunar Alps

Mons Pico

Archimedes Crater

Sea of Serenity

Sea of Crises

Kepler Crater

Sea of Vapors

Sea of Tranquillity

Ocean of Storms

Sea of Fertility

Sea of Clouds

PTOLEMAEUS CRATER
This crater has a diameter of approximately 100 miles (164 km). You would have to walk for longer than a day to cross it on foot.

32

STRAIGHT WALL
This cliff is 80 miles (130 km) long and 780 feet (240 m) high. It is also known by its Latin name, *Rupes Recta*.

THE MOON

The Moon is the Earth's only natural satellite. Although it may appear to be very bright, it does not shine with its own light but simply reflects light from the Sun. The surface of the Moon is gray, rocky, and very dusty. There is no air, wind, or atmosphere there, so things stay on the surface for a very long time. The Moon rotates on its axis in the same length of time that it takes to orbit the Earth. For this reason, you can always see the same side of the Moon from Earth. Many areas of the Moon's surface are called "seas"; however, there is not actually any water in them. Astronomers mistakenly thought they were areas of water, but eventually realized that was not the case. And the name just stuck!

LUNAR ECLIPSE
When the Earth is between the Sun and the Moon, and the three celestial bodies are aligned, the Sun shines on the Earth, and the Moon is in the Earth's shadow. This is a total lunar eclipse. The Moon does not disappear completely because a little of the Sun's light shines through Earth's atmosphere and is scattered onto the Moon. This makes the Moon look red, and is often called a "blood moon." If the alignment of the three bodies is not perfect, the Earth's shadow only partially obscures the Moon; this is a partial eclipse.

SEA OF MOSCOW
This "sea" was the subject of the first photograph of the hidden side of the Moon, taken by the Russian probe Luna 3. It was named after the city, Moscow.

Campbell Crater

LUNAR PHASES
Every night the Moon looks different. It is still the same moon, but because of the way the Sun shines on it, sometimes we can only see part of it. Which part the Sun shines on depends on where the Moon is in relation to the Earth. These shapes are called lunar phases.

Mendeleev Crater

CORDILLERA MOUNTAINS
This large mountain range runs around the edge of the Eastern Sea.

EASTERN SEA
This "sea" has three circular mountain ranges, which are located around each other. It has a large 150-mile (250-km) plain in its center, making it look like a bull's-eye.

Gagarin Crater

Korolev Crater

Apollo Crater

SOUTH POLE – AITKEN BASIN
This is one of the largest impact craters that we have found in the solar system. It has a diameter of 1,400 miles (2,240 km), which is more than the distance between New York and Dallas, Texas. It is located near the Moon's south pole.

Sea of Cleverness

SELENEAN SUMMIT
The highest point on the Moon is 35,387 feet (10,786 m). This is higher than Mount Everest, the tallest mountain on Earth, which stands at 29,029 feet (8,848 m) tall.

New Moon

Waxing Crescent

First Quarter

Waxing Gibbous

Full Moon

Waning Gibbous

Last Quarter

Waning Crescent

33

IDENTITY CARD

THE MOON

DISTANCE FROM EARTH	Average 238,900 miles (384,400 km)
DIAMETER	2,159 miles (3,476 km); a little more than a quarter of Earth's diameter
TIME OF REVOLUTION	27 days and 8 hours
TIME OF ROTATION	27 days and 8 hours
AVERAGE TEMPERATURE	From 250°F (120°C) to −330°F (−200°C)
GRAVITY	One sixth that of Earth (you weigh six times less on the Moon)

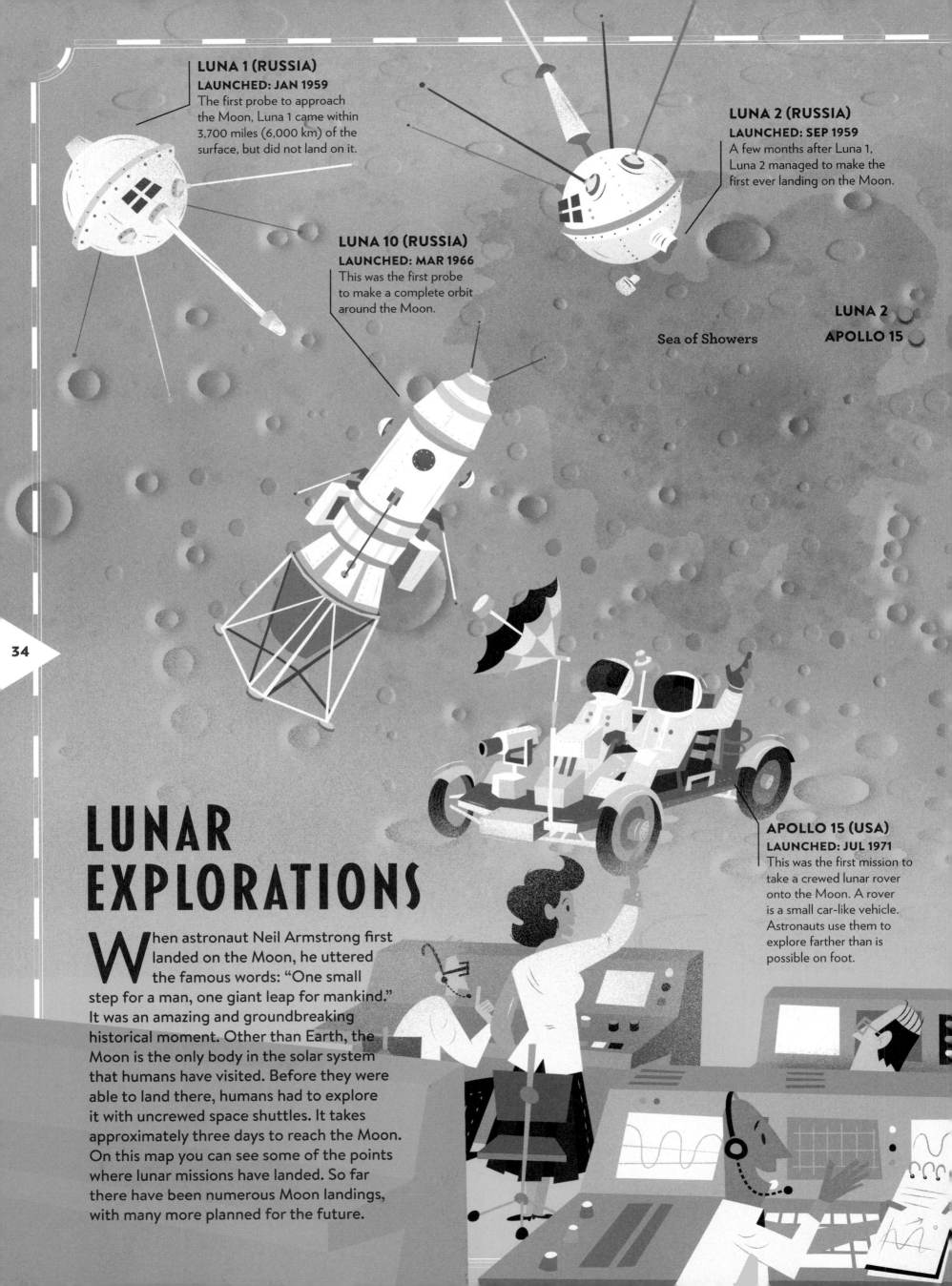

LUNA 1 (RUSSIA)
LAUNCHED: JAN 1959
The first probe to approach the Moon, Luna 1 came within 3,700 miles (6,000 km) of the surface, but did not land on it.

LUNA 2 (RUSSIA)
LAUNCHED: SEP 1959
A few months after Luna 1, Luna 2 managed to make the first ever landing on the Moon.

LUNA 10 (RUSSIA)
LAUNCHED: MAR 1966
This was the first probe to make a complete orbit around the Moon.

Sea of Showers

LUNA 2
APOLLO 15

APOLLO 15 (USA)
LAUNCHED: JUL 1971
This was the first mission to take a crewed lunar rover onto the Moon. A rover is a small car-like vehicle. Astronauts use them to explore farther than is possible on foot.

LUNAR EXPLORATIONS

When astronaut Neil Armstrong first landed on the Moon, he uttered the famous words: "One small step for a man, one giant leap for mankind." It was an amazing and groundbreaking historical moment. Other than Earth, the Moon is the only body in the solar system that humans have visited. Before they were able to land there, humans had to explore it with uncrewed space shuttles. It takes approximately three days to reach the Moon. On this map you can see some of the points where lunar missions have landed. So far there have been numerous Moon landings, with many more planned for the future.

LUNA 3 (RUSSIA)
LAUNCHED: OCT 1959
This probe took the first photograph of the hidden face of the Moon.

LUNA 21 (RUSSIA)
LAUNCHED: JAN 1973
This uncrewed mission took a rover onto the Moon. The rover accidentally shut down five months into the mission. Unfortunately it could not be recovered, and it is still there today.

LUNA 21
Sea of Serenity

Sea of Tranquillity

APOLLO 11

APOLLO 13 (USA)
LAUNCHED: APR 1970
"Houston, we've had a problem..." This is the famous quote from astronaut Jack Swigert. He uttered the words on the Apollo 13 mission when he realized his shuttle was in trouble. This should have been the third mission to land on the Moon, but an explosion damaged the shuttle. The astronauts had to abort the mission and return home to Earth.

APOLLO 11 (USA)
LAUNCHED: JUL 1969
This mission took Neil Armstrong and Edwin "Buzz" Aldrin to the Moon. They became the first people to land on the surface. There is no air, rain, or wind on the Moon, so Armstrong's footprints are still there. And the flag that they put up on the surface of the Moon never flaps!

EXPLORING THE MOON

Each mission to the Moon has had its own goals. The Luna missions' objective was to get close to the Moon and land a craft to collect rock samples. The Ranger missions were sent to capture as many images as possible. The first controlled landings on the Moon were completed by the Surveyor missions, and their probes took lots of photos. So far, probes have managed to photograph 99% of the surface. The Apollo missions were the first to send people to our celestial neighbor.

Make sure you keep up with our alien guide—this might be a bumpy ride!

WHAT ARE OTHER PLANETS LIKE?

All of the planets in our solar system can be seen from Earth with a telescope. You can even see some of them with just the naked eye. Planets can often look like stars because of the way that they reflect light from the Sun. Humans cannot live on most of the other planets in our solar system because the planets do not have the right conditions to support life. But they are still fascinating. Let's go planet-hopping!

NORTH POLE

The temperature ranges from −290°F (−180°C) to −150°F (−99°C) on Mercury's poles. The craters here are always in shade, and it is believed that they may have reserves of ice.

NO ATMOSPHERE

Mercury has almost no atmosphere, so there is nothing to trap heat from the Sun. During the day, Mercury's surface reaches extremely high temperatures. The surface temperature can then drop to far below freezing when the Sun goes down.

Pantheon Fossae

Schiaparelli Dorsum

Atget Crater

CALORIS BASIN

This is the largest crater on Mercury, with a diameter of 960 miles (1,550 km). It is surrounded by rings of mountains up to 6,500 feet (2 km) high. Its internal surface is covered with a layer of solidified lava.

Mozart Crater

TOLSTOY CRATER

This is an impact crater with a diameter of approximately 250 miles (400 km). It is surrounded by a double ring of mountains.

Basho Crater

DOSTOEVSKY CRATER

This enormous impact crater takes its name from a famous Russian author. And it is not the only place on Mercury named after a famous person. Can you spot any others on the map?

MERCURY, THE SUN'S NEIGHBOR

Mercury is the smallest rocky planet in the solar system—it is only as wide as the Atlantic Ocean on Earth. Although it is tiny, it travels really fast around the Sun. That is why it was named after the Roman god Mercury, who was a super-speedy messenger. It is not a very hospitable planet; there is no air or water there and, like the Moon, it is covered in craters. Mercury has almost no atmosphere and therefore is not able to stop meteors crashing into it. These maps show a few of the most interesting craters.

IDENTITY CARD

MERCURY

TYPE OF PLANET	Rocky
POSITION FROM THE SUN	1st planet, at 28.6 million miles (57.9 million km)
DIAMETER	3,032 miles (4,879 km)
TIME OF REVOLUTION	88 days
TIME OF ROTATION	59 days
AVERAGE TEMPERATURE	332°F (167°C)
MOONS	0

ANTONIADI DORSUM AND SCHIAPARELLI DORSUM

These two ridges on opposite sides of the planet reach a height of 13,000 feet (4 km). The features take their names from the astronomers who discovered them.

FULLER CRATER

This crater is never exposed to the Sun. It is covered with mysterious dark and light material. Astronomers think that it was probably created by an impact with an enormous frozen rock. The light patches may be ice that never melted.

Antoniadi Dorsum

Proust Crater

Giotto Crater

Tchaikovsky Crater

Titian Crater

Calvino Crater

Homer Crater

Ravel Crater

Murasaki Crater

Ibsen Crater

KUIPER CRATER

Sitting just above the Murasaki Crater is the Kuiper Crater. It is the only crater named after an astronomer—Gerard Kuiper. The rest are named after artists, writers, and composers.

MERCURY SCARPS

Mercury is full of holes and crevices. And its surface is dotted with tall cliffs called scarps. These cliffs were formed when the outer layer of the planet cracked and areas rose up along these fractures. This is just like what happens when you bake a cake: the crust will often crack and some of the still-hot contents spill out of the top.

A DOT ON THE SUN

Mercury is located between the Sun and the Earth. When the three bodies are aligned, it is possible to see Mercury as a little black dot moving across the Sun. This happens around 13 times every century (100 years). Venus does the same thing. Remember never to look directly at the Sun; it is so bright that it could damage your eyes, so you must always wear special eye protection.

ISHTAR TERRA

The smaller of two large highland areas, Ishtar Terra is bigger than Australia and includes the highest plateau (Lakshmi Planum) and the highest mountains (Maxwell Montes).

SPINNING BACKWARDS

Venus spins in the opposite direction from most other planets—it rotates clockwise, from east to west. So if you see the Sun rise from the west and set in the east, you might be on Venus. On Earth the Sun rises in the east and sets in the west.

Maxwell Montes

Fortuna Tessera

LAKSHMI PLANUM

This plateau (area of flat land that is high up) sits atop a large mountain range. Scientists believe that the mountains were formed by tectonic plates (large, moving pieces of rock) that crashed into each other. This caused the surrounding areas to buckle and rise up.

Sif Mons

Gula Mons

Mead Crater

Heng-o Corona

MYLITTA FLUCTUS

This is one of the largest lava flow fields on Venus. It is 620 miles (1,000 km) long and 290 miles (460 km) wide. It was made by a volcano that erupted and covered the land with lava, which eventually hardened.

Dione Regio

Eve Corona

ALPHA REGIO

Some volcanoes, like those in the Alpha Regio region, have a swollen center. This makes them look sort of like pancakes. These features were probably formed when thick molten lava cooled into solid rock.

VENUS, THE DAZZLING PLANET

Venus is located between Mercury and Earth. It is visible from Earth before sunrise and after sunset during certain times of the year. It is so dazzling that it was named after the Roman goddess of beauty. Venus is so bright because it is surrounded by a thick layer of cloud that reflects the light of the Sun. Venus's atmosphere is mostly made up of carbon dioxide and other gases. It also has very strong winds—up to 430 miles (700 km) per hour, which is faster than a tornado—and it is extremely hot.

IDENTITY CARD

VENUS

TYPE OF PLANET	Rocky
POSITION FROM THE SUN	2nd planet, at approximately 67 million miles (108 million km)
DIAMETER	7,520 miles (12,104 km)
TIME OF REVOLUTION	225 days
TIME OF ROTATION	243 days
AVERAGE TEMPERATURE	860°F (470°C)
MOONS	0

BALTIS VALLIS
At 4,200 miles (6,800 km) long, this is the longest lava channel in the whole of the solar system. It is thought that it once held a river of molten lava.

GOLUBKINA CRATER
This crater was named after Russian sculptor Anna Golubkina. After the initial meteorite impact, the internal cavity collapsed, leaving a deep hole. Some scientists thought that the hole seemed as though it had been made by the hand of a sculptor.

Volcanoes of the Niobe Planitia

SAPAS MONS
Similar to the volcanoes found on Hawaii, Sapas Mons is an enormous volcanic mountain. Its caldera (hollow area in the top) has a diameter of more than 250 miles (400 km)!

APHRODITE TERRA
This highland area is approximately the size of South America, and it appears to have large cracks.

DIANA CHASMA
This canyon is extraordinarily big. It is 1.9 miles (2.9 km) deep and 170 miles (280 km) long—that's the same length as Belgium!

41

Artemis Chasma

EARTH'S TWIN
Venus and Earth have lots of things in common. They are similar in size and have similar mass. It is thought that they were both formed from the same type of rock at the beginning of the solar system. Although Venus does have an atmosphere, we now know that it is too poisonous for humans to live there.

A VOLCANIC PLANET
The surface of Venus is mostly level and a yellow-reddish color. It has very few large craters. Its thick atmosphere is able to block and slow down any asteroids headed for the surface. Venus has more volcanoes than any other planet in the solar system. There are at least 156 large volcanoes plus many other smaller ones. It is also possible to find vast plains and riverbeds where lava once flowed, before it cooled and turned to solid rock.

NORTH POLE
The poles on Mars are covered in ice, similar to the polar ice caps on Earth. The size of these ice caps varies depending on the season and temperature.

OLYMPUS MONS
This is the highest volcano and mountain on Mars. It is over 82,000 feet (25 km) high, with a diameter of around 370 miles (600 km).

Chryse Planitia

Cydonia

Ares Vallis

VALLES MARINERIS
This system of canyons is up to 1,900 miles (3,000 km) long, 370 miles (600 km) wide, and 5 miles (8 km) deep. If it were on the Earth, it would stretch farther than the length of the USA.

ARSIA MONS AND ITS CAVES
On the Arsia Mons volcano, which is 62,000 feet (19 km) high, there are as many as seven enormous and dark caverns.

Deimos

Phobos

MARS, THE RED PLANET

Ancient Romans named this planet after Mars, their god of war, because the planet was red like blood. The real reason for its color is rust, which has formed on the planet because it is very rich in iron. Mars wouldn't make a great home for humans—it is a cold planet with a very thin atmosphere. Air there is mostly made up of carbon dioxide, which humans can't breathe. Like Mercury, Mars is also covered in lots of impact craters.

IDENTITY CARD

MARS

TYPE OF PLANET	Rocky
POSITION FROM THE SUN	4th planet, at 142 million miles (228 million km)
DIAMETER	4,222 miles (6,796 km)
TIME OF REVOLUTION	687 days
TIME OF ROTATION	1 day and 37 minutes
AVERAGE TEMPERATURE	−81°F (−63°C)
MOONS	2 (Deimos and Phobos)

THE MARTIAN SKY
The sky on Mars is not blue like it is on Earth, but an orange-pink color. This is because of the iron oxide powder that is suspended in the atmosphere.

NORTH POLAR BASIN
This impact crater has a diameter of over 6,200 miles (10,000 km) at its widest point, which means it is bigger than Asia, Europe, and Australia put together!

ATHABASCA VALLES AND CERBERUS PALUS
These swirls were formed by lava that erupted from the volcanoes. It flowed out at different speeds, causing faster flows to curl around slower ones.

SYRTIS MAJOR PLANUM
This is a volcanic region that stretches for over 930 miles (1,500 km).

Gale Crater

ELYSIUM PLANITIA
This area is south of the second-largest volcanic region on Mars, and may be covered by a frozen sea.

CERBERUS FOSSAE
These cracks in the crust of Mars were probably caused by lava flowing up from below.

43

RECORD-BREAKING PLANET
Olympus Mons is the highest mountain not only on Mars, but on any planet in the solar system. It is three times as high as Mount Everest—the tallest mountain on Earth. Mars also has the largest crater in the solar system. Called Hellas Planitia, it was formed by the huge impact of a comet or an asteroid.

THE MYTH OF THE MARTIANS
In 1877 the Italian astronomer Schiaparelli was the first to draw a map of Mars. He described a series of dark lines that he thought he saw on the surface. He called them *canali*, which is the Italian word for "channels." This word was mistranslated into "canals," which made people believe that Martian beings had dug canals on Mars! No trace of life has yet been found on Mars, but the myth of extraterrestrials from the planet continues.

PHOENIX

PHOENIX (USA)
This spacecraft arrived on Mars in 2008 to look for ice. After only five months, its solar panels stopped working. NASA was unable to make contact with it. Nearly ten years later, a satellite took a photo of the wreck of the poor Phoenix.

Chryse Planitia

Olympus Mons

MARS PATHFINDER

Ares Vallis

VIKING 1

VIKING 1 & 2 (USA)
Launched in 1975, these probes took many color images of Mars. They measured temperatures at their landing sites and found that they were all below freezing. These space robots had arms and were able to collect samples from the ground.

OPPORTUNITY

Arsia Mons

Valles Marineris

EXPLORING MARS

Humans have been sending probes to explore Mars since the 1960s. The Mariner 4 probe came within 6,118 miles (9,846 km) of Mars and took the first photographs of the planet. Since then, all sorts of probes have been sent: orbiters, landers (probes that land on the planet), and rovers (small space vehicles). Going to Mars, however, is not at all easy, and many of the missions have failed. Humans haven't yet walked on the red planet, but many space agencies plan to. On November 26, 2018, NASA's InSight probe arrived on Mars, and it has been sending back daily weather reports from the planet ever since.

MARINER 4 (USA)
This was the first probe to fly to Mars and was launched in 1964. Mariner 4 found a planet with lots of craters and a much thinner and less dense atmosphere than was expected. The probe took photographs, which showed that there was no life or liquid water on Mars. However, they did show deep craters and valleys.

44

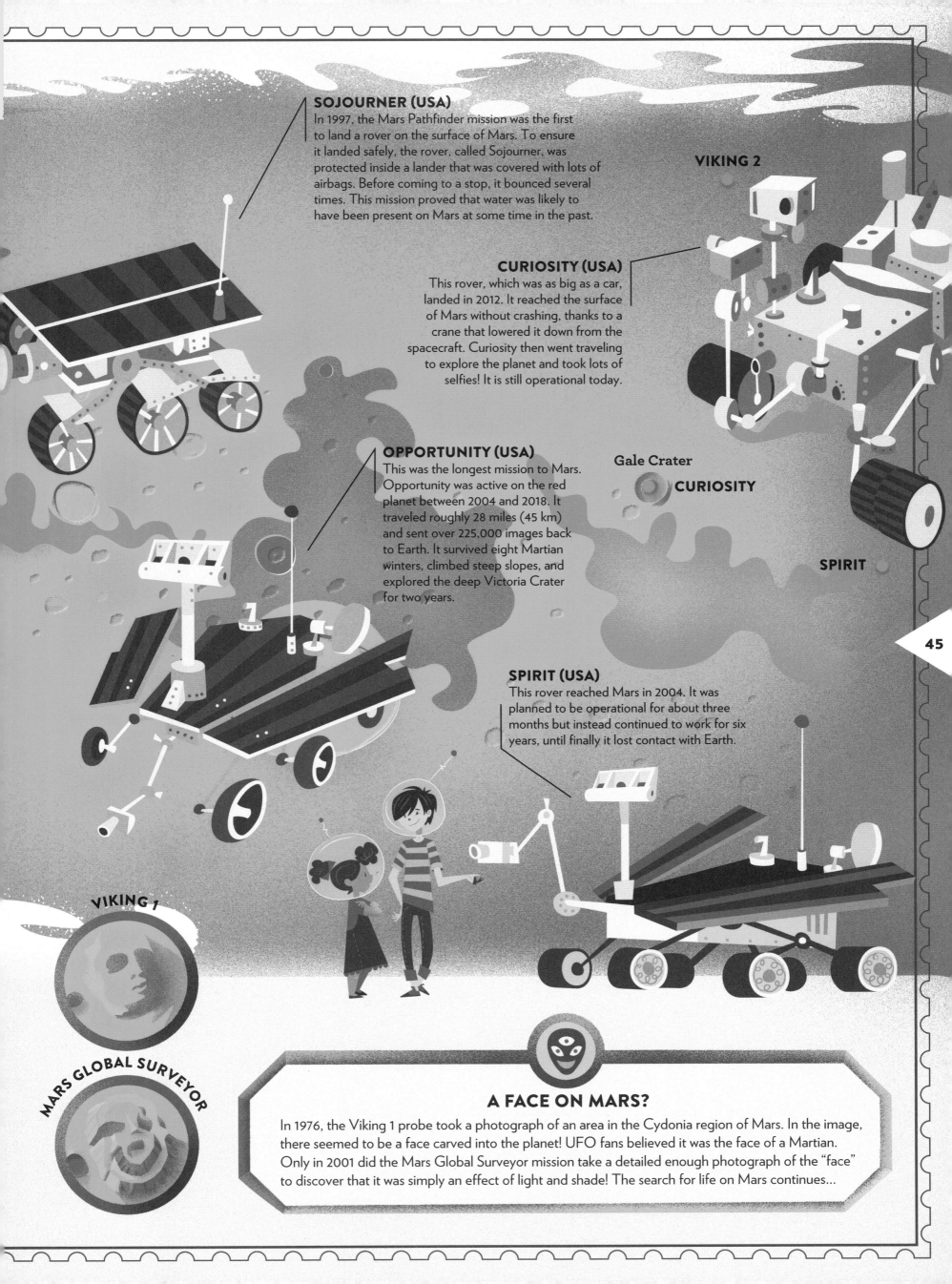

SOJOURNER (USA)

In 1997, the Mars Pathfinder mission was the first to land a rover on the surface of Mars. To ensure it landed safely, the rover, called Sojourner, was protected inside a lander that was covered with lots of airbags. Before coming to a stop, it bounced several times. This mission proved that water was likely to have been present on Mars at some time in the past.

VIKING 2

CURIOSITY (USA)

This rover, which was as big as a car, landed in 2012. It reached the surface of Mars without crashing, thanks to a crane that lowered it down from the spacecraft. Curiosity then went traveling to explore the planet and took lots of selfies! It is still operational today.

OPPORTUNITY (USA)

This was the longest mission to Mars. Opportunity was active on the red planet between 2004 and 2018. It traveled roughly 28 miles (45 km) and sent over 225,000 images back to Earth. It survived eight Martian winters, climbed steep slopes, and explored the deep Victoria Crater for two years.

Gale Crater

CURIOSITY

SPIRIT

45

SPIRIT (USA)

This rover reached Mars in 2004. It was planned to be operational for about three months but instead continued to work for six years, until finally it lost contact with Earth.

VIKING 1

MARS GLOBAL SURVEYOR

A FACE ON MARS?

In 1976, the Viking 1 probe took a photograph of an area in the Cydonia region of Mars. In the image, there seemed to be a face carved into the planet! UFO fans believed it was the face of a Martian. Only in 2001 did the Mars Global Surveyor mission take a detailed enough photograph of the "face" to discover that it was simply an effect of light and shade! The search for life on Mars continues...

MAGNETIC FIELD

Jupiter has a spinning metallic core. This spinning causes the planet to have a strong magnetic field that is similar to Earth's. But while on Earth a compass points north, on Jupiter it would point south.

POLAR CYCLONES

It is not possible to get close to the poles on Jupiter. This is because there are terrible cyclones there. In fact there is a central cyclone over each pole, surrounded by other cyclones of similar size. The winds here reach 225 miles (350 km) per hour.

JUPITER, THE GIANT AMONG PLANETS

Jupiter is the largest planet in the solar system. It has a diameter 11 times that of the Earth. And its volume is so great that it could contain 1,300 Earths. Gravity is so strong on Jupiter that a person who weighs 150 pounds (70 kg) on Earth would weigh 385 pounds (175 kg) there. Because of its super-strength gravity, Jupiter can affect the orbit of asteroids, disrupt the movement of other planets, and even attract comets. This map of Jupiter is different from the maps of the other planets that we have already seen. It doesn't show two sides of the planet, only one. This is because Jupiter is a gaseous planet and so is always moving. No side is ever the same. Because it has no hard surface, it is impossible to walk on Jupiter or to send landers or rovers there. There are no mountains, volcanoes, or craters—only dense clouds and raging storms.

Warning: You can't walk on Jupiter—you would sink!

JUPITER

IDENTITY CARD

TYPE OF PLANET	Gaseous
POSITION FROM THE SUN	5th planet, at 484 million miles (778 million km)
DIAMETER	86,881 miles (142,984 km)
TIME OF REVOLUTION	12 years
TIME OF ROTATION	10 hours
AVERAGE TEMPERATURE	−234°F (−145°C)
MOONS	79

POLAR AURORAS

On Earth there are natural lights called auroras in the sky around the north and south poles. These are commonly known as the Northern and Southern Lights. They are caused by particles from the Sun that react with the Earth's atmosphere. Jupiter also has auroras, and they are up to 10 times brighter than those on Earth. Scientists think that the particles responsible for Jupiter's polar auroras come from one of Jupiter's moons, Io.

THE GREAT RED SPOT

There is an area of Jupiter that looks like an enormous red eye. In fact, it is a gigantic hurricane. It is 10,000 miles (16,000 km) wide. That's bigger than the entire Earth! It is also very deep and appears to stretch for up to 200 miles (300 km) inside the surface of the planet. It has been visible for at least 200 years.

HALO RING

This thin ring stretches to the edge of the planet's atmosphere.

MAIN RING

This is the thinnest ring of all, stretching to about 4,000 miles (6,000 km).

GOSSAMER RING

This ring is located about 80,000 miles (129,000 km) above the planet's clouds. It is 60,000 miles (97,000 km) wide and is the outermost and the faintest of the rings.

A STRIPED PLANET

Jupiter is a striped planet. Some of the stripes are approximately 19,000 miles (30,000 km) wide. That's more than twice the entire diameter of the Earth. The stripes are caused by the clouds that surround Jupiter and have hardly changed for the last 100 years. They have bright and dark areas and extend into the planet for thousands of miles. You can even see the stripes of Jupiter from Earth if you use a telescope.

THE RINGS OF JUPITER

Jupiter is surrounded by faint rings of dust. The Voyager 1 probe took photographs of these rings in 1979, and there appear to be three main sections. The names of the sections are Gossamer, Main, and Halo Rings. Each one has a reddish-orange or blue color and is several miles thick. The dust in the rings came from some of Jupiter's moons, which collided with other space objects. The dust was then pulled into orbit by Jupiter's gravity.

JUPITER'S MOONS

Over 400 years ago, the astronomer Galileo Galilei observed four moons around Jupiter: Io, Europa, Callisto, and Ganymede. With his simple telescope, he just saw them as tiny dots around the planet. When he saw that they moved, he understood that those dots must be in orbit around Jupiter. This caused many people to become outraged—why does Jupiter have four moons, but Earth only have one? We now know that Jupiter actually has at least 79 moons! Let's have a close look at the first four moons that Galileo discovered.

TYRE CRATER
This impact crater is a gigantic series of rings. It is thought that there could perhaps be liquid water below the surface.

Europa

PWYLL CRATER
This crater has a diameter of approximately 15 miles (25 km) and a chain of hills in the center. It is the youngest impact crater on the surface of Europa.

GEYSERS
It appears that there are geysers on Europa's surface, which blast out jets of vapor. The vapor most likely originates in a warm underground sea. This means that there could be life on this moon.

BOÖSAULE MONTES
These mountains have three peaks with bases on a plateau that is more than 300 miles (500 km) high. The highest peak is South Boösaule Montes.

Io

PELE
This is an active volcano on Io's surface. Passing spacecraft have spotted a tall volcanic plume erupting from it.

LOKI PATERA
This "hole" on the surface of Io is a gigantic lava lake. Astronomers have even identified waves on it, very similar to those in our seas.

EUBOEA MONTES
This tall, sloping mountain is more than 33,000 feet (10,000 m) high, which is around the same height as Mauna Kea on Earth.

IO
This is the closest of the four moons to Jupiter. It is rich in active volcanoes (approximately 150 of Io's 400 volcanoes are active) from which lava continuously erupts. As there is very little gravity, the debris and the lava rise up to 190 miles (300 km) in the air in extraordinary eruptions. There are also some very high mountains on Io.

EUROPA
The surface of Europa is covered in ice, which reflects the Sun's rays like a mirror. The force of Jupiter's gravity caused Europa's ice crust to crack. The crust then solidified again, leaving some lighter lines on the surface. This has made scientists think that there may be liquid water on this moon and therefore that the presence of life is possible.

GIPUL CATENA
This area is a long series of linked impact catenae (chains of craters) in a straight line. It was probably caused by a collision with a comet.

EGDIR CRATER
This crater has a diameter of 37 miles (60 km). That's about 600 times the length of a soccer field.

GALILEO REGIO
This dark terrain was named after Galileo Galilei, who discovered Ganymede.

POLAR AURORAS
Scientists have studied the polar auroras around Ganymede and have found patterns in it. This hints to the existence of a deep salt sea under its surface.

Callisto

Ganymede

VALHALLA BASIN
This basin is the largest multi-ring impact crater in the solar system. It stretches over 1,800 miles (3,000 km). The basin was named after a grand hall belonging to the god Odin in Norse mythology.

MIMIR CRATER
This crater was named after a giant from Norse mythology and stretches for approximately 30 miles (50 km).

49

URUK SULCUS
This is a deeply grooved area that separates Galileo Regio from Marius Regio.

MARIUS REGIO
This geological feature is an area of ancient, dark land.

OSIRIS CRATER
This crater is relatively young and is surrounded by bright, icy material.

GANYMEDE
This is the largest moon in the solar system. It is even bigger than Mercury! If it were in orbit around the Sun, it would be classified as a planet, but as it orbits Jupiter, it is classified as a moon. Though 40% of its surface is dark and full of craters, the remaining 60% is light and full of ridges.

CALLISTO
The surface of Callisto is covered in rocks, ice, and craters. It has the highest number of multi-ring impact craters and ridges in the solar system. The brightest points on the map show just a few of the many impact craters that dot its surface.

THE RINGS OF SATURN

It is thought that the pieces of rock and ice that make up Saturn's rings were once a moon. It could either have collided with a comet or asteroid or have been ripped apart by Saturn's gravitational force. The chunks were then pulled into orbit around the planet. The ring system is very narrow, with a thickness of only 30 feet (10 m) in parts. However, it stretches up to 175,000 miles (282,000 km) from the planet. The rings are named alphabetically in the order that they were discovered.

Like Jupiter, Saturn's magnetic field is opposite to Earth's.

A RING

This is the outermost of the large rings. It is between 30 and 100 feet (10 and 30 m) thick.

BANDED ATMOSPHERE

Saturn is covered in a blanket of clouds that circle around it in bands. The clouds move at different speeds, which creates stripes. The pressure in Saturn's atmosphere is so high that it can squeeze gas into liquid. Spacecraft would not be able to enter the atmosphere and survive.

ENCKE GAP

This gap in Saturn's A ring is caused by the moon Pan, which orbits the planet within it.

CASSINI DIVISION

This large, empty space spans the area between Saturn's A and B rings. It was discovered by Giovanni Cassini in 1675.

50

SATURN, THE LORD OF THE RINGS

One of the main characteristics of Saturn is its ring system. The first person to find the rings was the astronomer Galileo Galilei. When he first saw them, he compared them to a donkey's ears because they stuck out on both sides of the planet! Every 15 years, when Saturn's rings are edge-on to Earth, we can't see them. Because they are very thin, they are very difficult to detect from the side. However, if you were to see them from above, they would be hard to miss, as they stretch for many thousands of miles. Saturn does not have a solid crust and it is a lot less dense than the Earth. This low density means that if it were in water, it would float!

SATURN

TYPE OF PLANET	Gaseous
POSITION FROM THE SUN	6th planet, at 886 million miles (1,429 million km)
DIAMETER	72,367 miles (116,464 km)
TIME OF REVOLUTION	29 years
TIME OF ROTATION	10 hours and 14 minutes
AVERAGE TEMPERATURE	−290°F (−180°C)
MOONS	At least 82

IDENTITY CARD

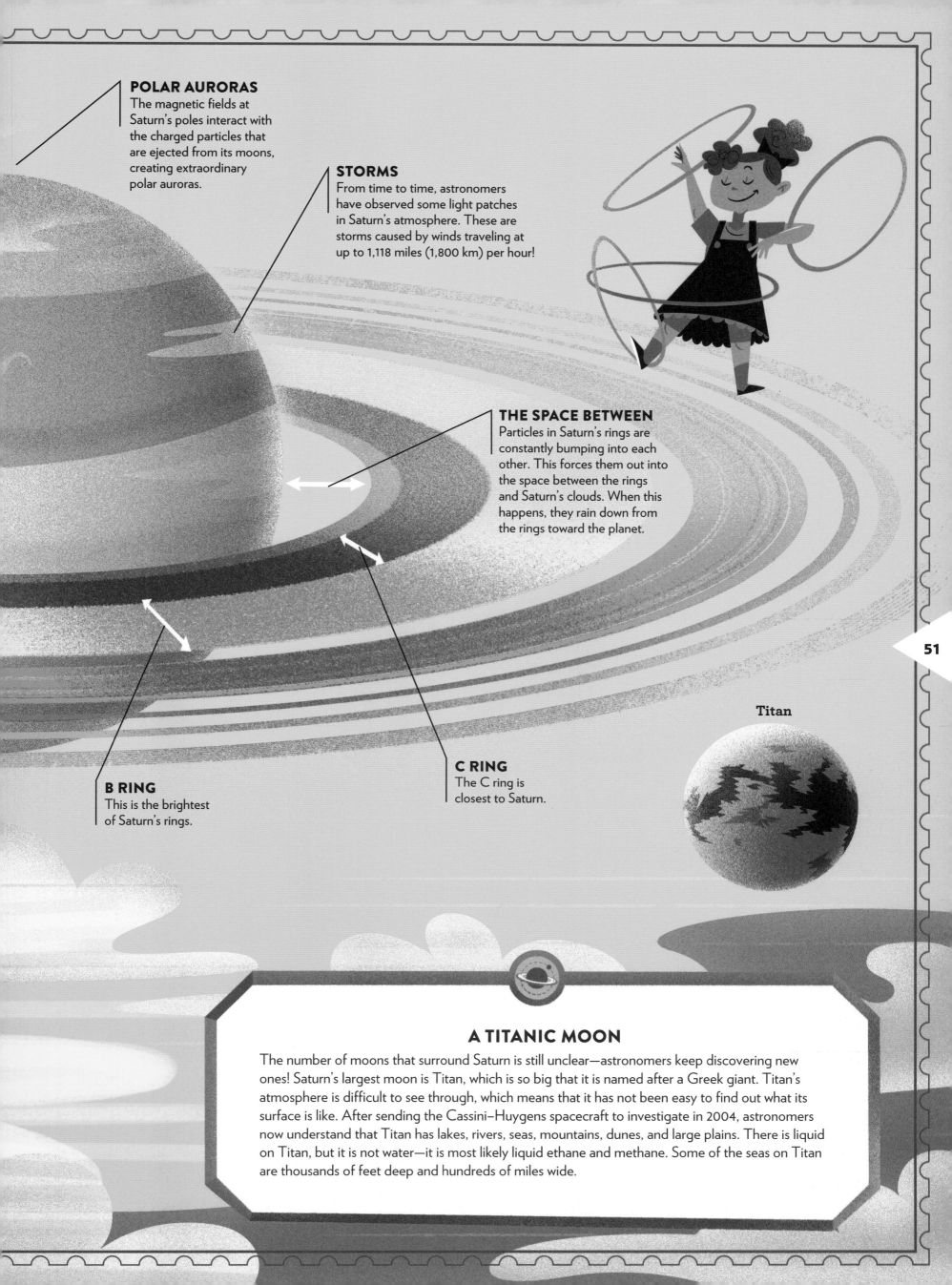

POLAR AURORAS
The magnetic fields at Saturn's poles interact with the charged particles that are ejected from its moons, creating extraordinary polar auroras.

STORMS
From time to time, astronomers have observed some light patches in Saturn's atmosphere. These are storms caused by winds traveling at up to 1,118 miles (1,800 km) per hour!

THE SPACE BETWEEN
Particles in Saturn's rings are constantly bumping into each other. This forces them out into the space between the rings and Saturn's clouds. When this happens, they rain down from the rings toward the planet.

B RING
This is the brightest of Saturn's rings.

C RING
The C ring is closest to Saturn.

Titan

A TITANIC MOON
The number of moons that surround Saturn is still unclear—astronomers keep discovering new ones! Saturn's largest moon is Titan, which is so big that it is named after a Greek giant. Titan's atmosphere is difficult to see through, which means that it has not been easy to find out what its surface is like. After sending the Cassini–Huygens spacecraft to investigate in 2004, astronomers now understand that Titan has lakes, rivers, seas, mountains, dunes, and large plains. There is liquid on Titan, but it is not water—it is most likely liquid ethane and methane. Some of the seas on Titan are thousands of feet deep and hundreds of miles wide.

IDENTITY CARD

URANUS

TYPE OF PLANET	Gaseous
POSITION FROM THE SUN	7th planet, at 1,786 million miles (2,875 million km)
DIAMETER	31,518 miles (50,724 km)
TIME OF REVOLUTION	84 years
TIME OF ROTATION	17 hours and 14 minutes
AVERAGE TEMPERATURE	−322°F (−197°C)
MOONS	At least 27

MOONS
The moons of Uranus are all named after characters from William Shakespeare's plays and Alexander Pope's poems.

Miranda

Cordelia

Ophelia

RINGS
The rings around Uranus are hard to see, so have been enhanced for this image. The ring that is farthest from the planet has a similar shape to the orbit of Mab, one of Uranus's moons.

WIND
Uranus has an atmosphere and very strong winds that can reach 560 miles (900 km) per hour!

Bianca

Mab

Juliet

Rosalind

Puck

Perdita

Cressida

Belinda

Desdemona

Cupid

Portia

URANUS, THE SIDEWAYS PLANET

Compared to the Earth, Uranus is enormous; it could contain 60 planets like ours. This planet is rich in methane gas, which is what gives it its blue color. It is a kingdom of ice and clouds. Uranus is far away from the Sun and extremely cold. Uranus is the only planet in our solar system that appears to be on its side. It could have been knocked this way by a collision with another large space object.

GREAT DARK SPOT

Do you remember Jupiter's Great Red Spot? Well, the Great Dark Spot on Neptune is very similar. It was discovered in 1989, but then it strangely disappeared. Years later, other, smaller ones popped up on the planet's surface.

WINDS AND CLOUDS

Winds on Neptune are faster than 1,200 miles (2,000 km) per hour. They are the strongest winds in the solar system, five times more violent than a hurricane on Earth.

RINGS

Neptune has five rings that are thin and not very visible. They have been enhanced for this image.

Triton

TRITON

This is a strange moon because it orbits the planet in the opposite direction from Neptune's orbit. This is called a retrograde orbit. Here the temperature goes down to −391°F (−235°C!) Brrr...

NEPTUNE, THE FROZEN PLANET

This planet is so blue that it almost looks as if it were covered by sea. This is the reason it was named after the Roman god of the sea. It is the planet that is farthest away from the Sun and has the coldest temperature on average in the entire solar system. Neptune is the only planet that is not visible from Earth without a telescope.

IDENTITY CARD

NEPTUNE

TYPE OF PLANET	Gaseous
POSITION FROM THE SUN	8th planet, at 2,793 million miles (4,504 million km)
DIAMETER	30,599 miles (49,244 km)
TIME OF REVOLUTION	165 years
TIME OF ROTATION	16 hours and 7 minutes
AVERAGE TEMPERATURE	−328°F (−200°C)
MOONS	At least 14

PLUTO

DUNES
Dunes have been spotted on Pluto. It is believed that they are made of frozen grains of methane.

Venera Terra

Voyager Terra

Pioneer Terra

SPUTNIK PLANITIA
This is a frozen plain that is mostly made of methane. Its basin is approximately 620 miles (1,000 km) wide and 2.5 miles (4 km) deep.

Viking Terra

Elliot Crater

Virgil Fossae

Beatrice Fossa

Cthulhu Macula

Hillary Montes

TENZING MONTES
This is the highest mountain range on Pluto, with a peak of over 20,000 feet (6,000 m), roughly the same height as Mount Kilimanjaro on Earth.

TOMBAUGH REGIO
This area is shaped like a heart. It is named after Clyde Tombaugh, who discovered Pluto in 1930.

PLUTO & CHARON

When it was first discovered, Pluto was classified as a planet. However, because of its relatively small size, it has since been reclassified as a dwarf planet. Pluto is one of five dwarf planets in our solar system. Most of them are found in the outer solar system, apart from Ceres, which is in the asteroid belt. Pluto is a cold place, with a frozen surface and a thin atmosphere. Scientists think the atmosphere is formed of methane, nitrogen, and carbon monoxide. Charon is Pluto's largest moon, and the two bodies are actually very similar in size. Charon's surface is made of frozen water.

OZ TERRA
This area with lots of craters takes its name from the famous children's novel *The Wonderful Wizard of Oz*.

MORDOR MACULA
Astronomers think that this spot is made of material that has been deposited on Charon from Pluto or one of its other moons. It is named after the place in J. R. R. Tolkien's *The Lord of the Rings* that is home to evil villain Sauron.

Dorothy Crater

Alice Crater

Spock Crater

Vulcan Planum

Sulu Crater

SERENITY CHASMA
This is part of a collection of chasms along Charon's equator. The belt of chasms stretches for over 1,000 miles (1,600 km).

KUBRICK MONS
This peak in a series of moon mountains is surrounded by a moat, or pit.

RULER OF THE UNDERWORLD
Pluto was given its name by an 11-year-old girl. She suggested to her grandfather that it should be named after the Roman god of the underworld because it was in such a cold, dark place. Her grandfather then told this to the observatory that was studying the planet and they agreed. One day on Pluto lasts approximately 153 Earth hours, while a complete revolution around the Sun, which is the duration of a Pluto year, would take 248 Earth years! Charon is the moon that we know the most about. But Pluto has five moons in total: Charon, Hydra, Nix, Kerberos, and Styx. Kerberos is named after the dog who guarded the underworld in Greek mythology.

OXO CRATER
This small 6-mile (10-km) crater is the second-brightest ice feature on Ceres.

HAULANI CRATER
This impact crater has a pitted plain inside it, with a mountain at its center.

Ninsar
Crater

Kirnis
Crater

Rongo
Crater

Kait
Crater

OCCATOR CRATER
This crater appears to be brighter than the others because there are two bright, icy features within it.

Hatipowa
Crater

Uhola
Catenae

56

CERES

Most asteroids rotate around the Sun in the main asteroid belt, which lies between Mars and Jupiter. The largest asteroid found here is Ceres. It has a diameter of 600 miles (972 km), and it was the first object in the asteroid belt to be discovered over 200 years ago. Since 2006, Ceres has been considered to be a dwarf planet, just like Pluto. Ceres is covered in craters. These maps highlight a few of the most curious craters that Ceres has to offer.

DANTU CRATER
This crater has a diameter of 78 miles (126 km) and is covered in rifts, or cracks. It has a depth of 3 miles (4.7 km) from its highest point to the bottom of the central pit.

Laukumate
Crater

SHINING BRIGHT
For years, nobody could understand why the craters on Ceres were so bright. They seemed to be full of a strange white substance. Today scientists believe that there is a concentration of salt or ice inside the craters.

Megwomets
Crater

Nawish
Crater

Rao
Crater

Cacaguat
Crater

Kumitoga
Crater

Fluusa
Crater

Toharu
Crater

JULING CRATER
It is believed that this crater contains water ice. Astronomers are always very interested in the presence of water, even if it is frozen as ice. Where there is water, there may be life.

KERWAN CRATER
This is the largest crater on Ceres. Kerwan crater is 174 miles (280 km) wide, and a smaller crater called Insitor sits inside it.

AN ARMY OF SMALL STONES

Asteroids come in many different sizes. There are around 1.9 million of them that are larger than 3,281 feet (1 km) in the main asteroid belt. But there are even more that are pebble-sized or smaller. If you put all of them together, you would end up with something just smaller than the Moon. Asteroids are not all the same. Some are made of rock, some of metal, and often they are dark in color because of the presence of carbon. When asteroids collide, they break into fragments, many of which have fallen to Earth as meteorites.

WHAT IS BEYOND OUR SOLAR SYSTEM?

Early telescopes could only show astronomers so much—they could see the skies strewn with stars and details on a few of the planets in our solar system. However, today's powerful telescopes can help astronomers see galaxies and more. Humans have now discovered incredible things in the space beyond our solar system. There are hundreds of millions of galaxies, shining nebulae, and glittering star clusters. Astronomers call these parts of distant sky "deep space."

THE SKY BEHIND URSA MAJOR

The Hubble Space Telescope is a super-powered telescope that scientists built to see deep into space. In 1995, it captured an image of a tiny section of sky (just 1 cm^2) located behind the constellation Ursa Major. The image was the most detailed portrait of space ever seen and was named the Hubble Deep Field. It helped scientists begin to understand how many galaxies could be in the universe. The picture was actually assembled from 342 separate images that were taken over ten days. Taking pictures of space isn't as easy as taking pictures of things on Earth. The light is very faint because it has to travel such a long way before it reaches the telescope.

1 cm^2

Alkaid

Mizar

Alioth

Megrez

Phad

Dubhe

Merak

60

TRAVELING THROUGH TIME

As we know, it takes a long time for light to travel through space—roughly one year to travel 6 trillion miles (9 trillion km). Therefore, this image is like looking back in time. It shows the galaxies as they were, possibly billions of years ago.

VERY DISTANT DOTS
The smallest dots in the image are the most distant galaxies. They are so far away that their light had been traveling for billions of years before the photo was taken.

OUR STARS
A few of the dots in the image are stars in our own galaxy, the Milky Way. They are much, much closer than the galaxies in the image.

SPIRAL GALAXIES
There are lots of spiral galaxies like our own in the image. It's strange to think that our Milky Way would look this small if seen from so far away.

ELLIPTICAL GALAXIES
Named for their shape, elliptical galaxies can be round or more of an elongated oval. They form these shapes because of the way that gas, dust, and stars move within them.

COLLIDING GALAXIES
The Hubble image shows many galaxies that are colliding or that had collided with each other in the past. When this happens, the result can be a single, much larger galaxy.

THE HUBBLE SPACE TELESCOPE
One thing that helps the Hubble Space Telescope see so far and clearly into space is that it is in orbit around the Earth. This means that its images are not distorted by Earth's atmosphere. It was launched into orbit around the Earth in 1990. Many astronauts have visited the telescope over the years to make repairs and add new instruments. Hubble has antennae so that it can communicate with and receive instructions from scientists on Earth. It generates electricity using solar panels that collect energy from the Sun.

THE SKY BEHIND ORION

This constellation can easily be seen without a telescope and is visible from everywhere in the world. It is named after Orion, a very large and strong hunter from Greek mythology. There are seven main stars that make up his core shape. Three stars represent his belt, two are his shoulders, and two are his knees. If you look at this constellation through a telescope, you will see that the area of sky around it is crowded with stars and nebulae.

1. PLANETARY NEBULA

Nebulae are created by dying stars, which expel gas at the end of their lives. This gas forms an illuminated shell around the stars. It is thought that there are around 10,000 planetary nebulae in the Milky Way.

2. HORSEHEAD NEBULA

Astronomers think that this nebula looks like the head of a horse. It appears to be quite dark because it contains a cloud of interstellar dust that blocks the light behind it. It is home to many young and extremely hot stars.

3. ORION NEBULA

This nebula is a stellar nursery—an area where new stars are born. It is so bright that it can be detected in the night sky without the use of a telescope. The Orion Nebula is the closest large star-forming region of space to Earth.

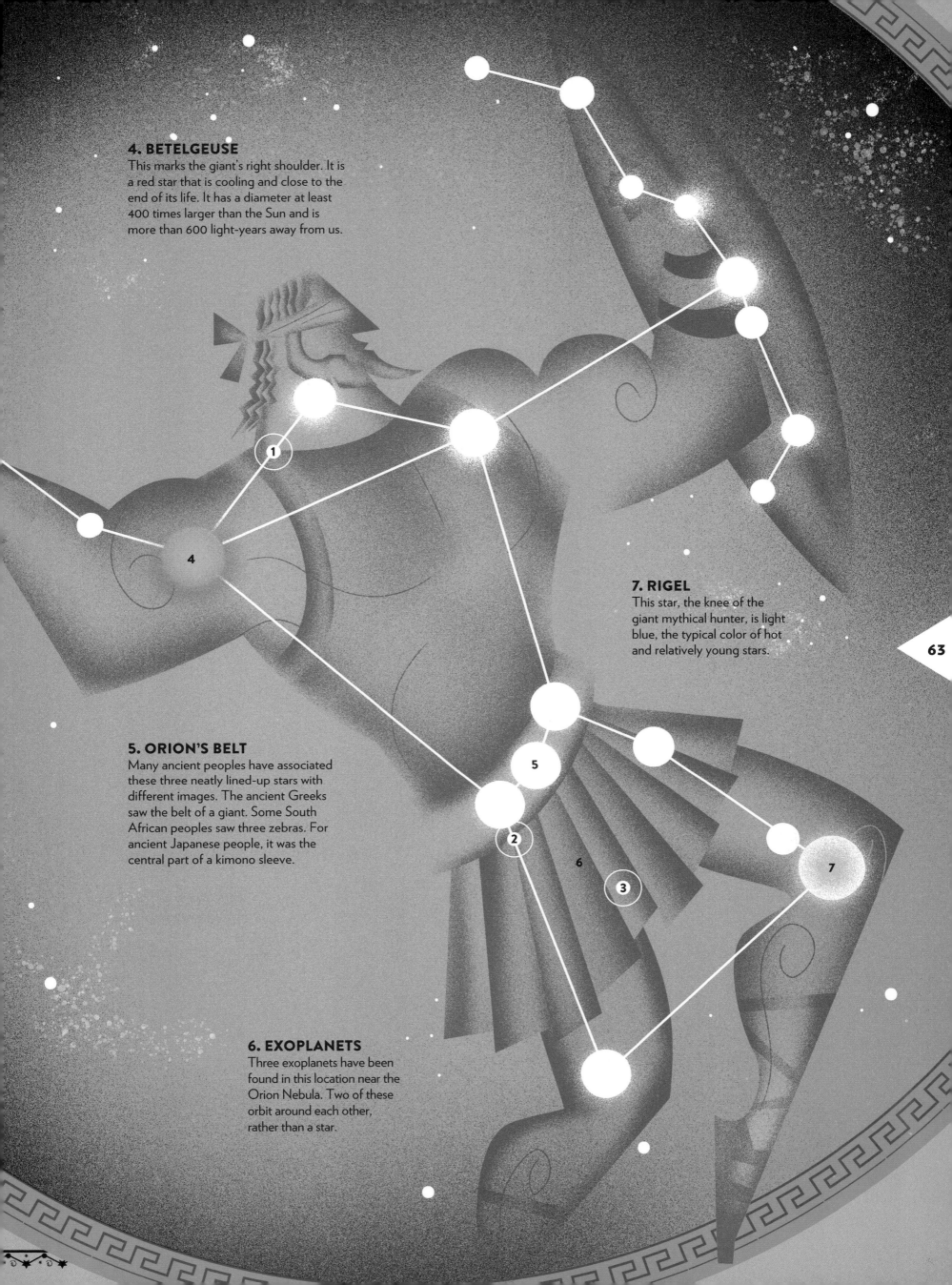

4. BETELGEUSE
This marks the giant's right shoulder. It is a red star that is cooling and close to the end of its life. It has a diameter at least 400 times larger than the Sun and is more than 600 light-years away from us.

7. RIGEL
This star, the knee of the giant mythical hunter, is light blue, the typical color of hot and relatively young stars.

5. ORION'S BELT
Many ancient peoples have associated these three neatly lined-up stars with different images. The ancient Greeks saw the belt of a giant. Some South African peoples saw three zebras. For ancient Japanese people, it was the central part of a kimono sleeve.

6. EXOPLANETS
Three exoplanets have been found in this location near the Orion Nebula. Two of these orbit around each other, rather than a star.

TARANTULA NEBULA

A nebula is an area of star formation and this particular one is named for its spiderlike shape. It stretches for more than 1,000 light-years.

NGC 2100

This is an open star cluster, which means that all of the stars in it are roughly the same age.

A SPACE SEAHORSE

Inside the star cluster NGC 2074, there is an area of dust that is shaped like a seahorse. It currently stretches for 20 light-years. However, scientists believe that in a few million years it will disappear.

THE LARGE MAGELLANIC CLOUD

The Large Magellanic Cloud (LMC) is a satellite galaxy of the Milky Way. This means that it rotates around the Milky Way. It includes around 10 billion stars as well as various nebulae and star clusters. It was named after the Portuguese explorer Ferdinand Magellan. He spotted it in 1519, while he was traveling around the world. However, the LMC was almost certainly known by those in the southern hemisphere many years before this date. In one Australian Aboriginal story the LMC is the campsite of an old man, and the Small Magellanic Cloud is the campsite of his wife.

HODGE 301
More than 40 stars have exploded as supernovae inside this cluster.

NGC 2070
Nestled in the Tarantula Nebula, this star cluster includes some of the largest stars ever observed. Many new stars are formed here.

NGC 2060
The brightest pulsar (a star that emits a pulsing beam of radiation) ever observed is located among this supernova remnant (material left over from a powerful stellar explosion).

SN 1987A
This supernova was the first to be observed with modern telescopes in 1987.

LARGE AND SMALL
The LMC is not alone. A similar, slightly smaller galaxy called the Small Magellanic Cloud can be seen nearby. Between the two there is a star-dust bridge called the Magellanic Bridge.

NGC 2074
This is a star cluster with an emission nebula, an area where clouds of gas are made to glow by a nearby hot star.

Dorado

Large Magellanic Cloud

WHERE IS IT?
The LMC is approximately 160,000 light-years away from Earth. However, there are other galaxies that are closer to us. The Sagittarius Galaxy is 87,000 light-years away. And the Canis Major Galaxy is 25,000 light-years away. The Large and Small Magellanic Clouds are two of only three galaxies that can be seen from the Earth without a telescope. The other is the Andromeda Galaxy.

THE CRAB NEBULA

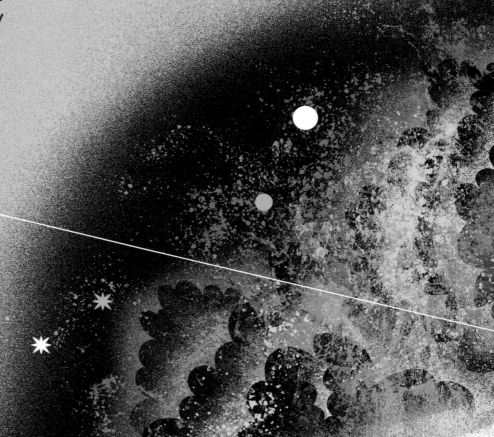

Way back in 1054, some Chinese and Arabian astronomers observed a new starlike object in the sky. Incredibly, they saw it during the day and without the use of a telescope. Many centuries later, it was discovered that in fact it was not a star. It was a supernova—an extraordinarily violent star explosion. The remnants of this explosion formed the Crab Nebula, which is still growing. The gases that it is made of are expanding at the speed of 930 miles (1,500 km) per second!

THE CRAB PULSAR
Inside the Crab Nebula there is a young neutron star, known as the Crab Pulsar. It spins at an extraordinary speed, completing 30 revolutions per second. The Crab Pulsar is extremely dense. It has a mass that is one and a half times that of the Sun. However, it is much smaller, with a diameter of only 12–19 miles (20–30 km). In spite of its small size, it produces 100,000 times more energy than our Sun.

A LIGHTHOUSE IN SPACE
Pulsars are similar to lighthouses. They transmit rays of radiation, which shine outward in two opposite directions as the pulsar spins. With their telescopes, astronomers can see these rays intermittently coming and going. This looks very similar to the light produced by a lighthouse.

EXPLOSION OF LIGHT
The destruction of the star caused such a huge explosion that the supernova shone super bright. This is why it could be seen in the daytime from Earth.

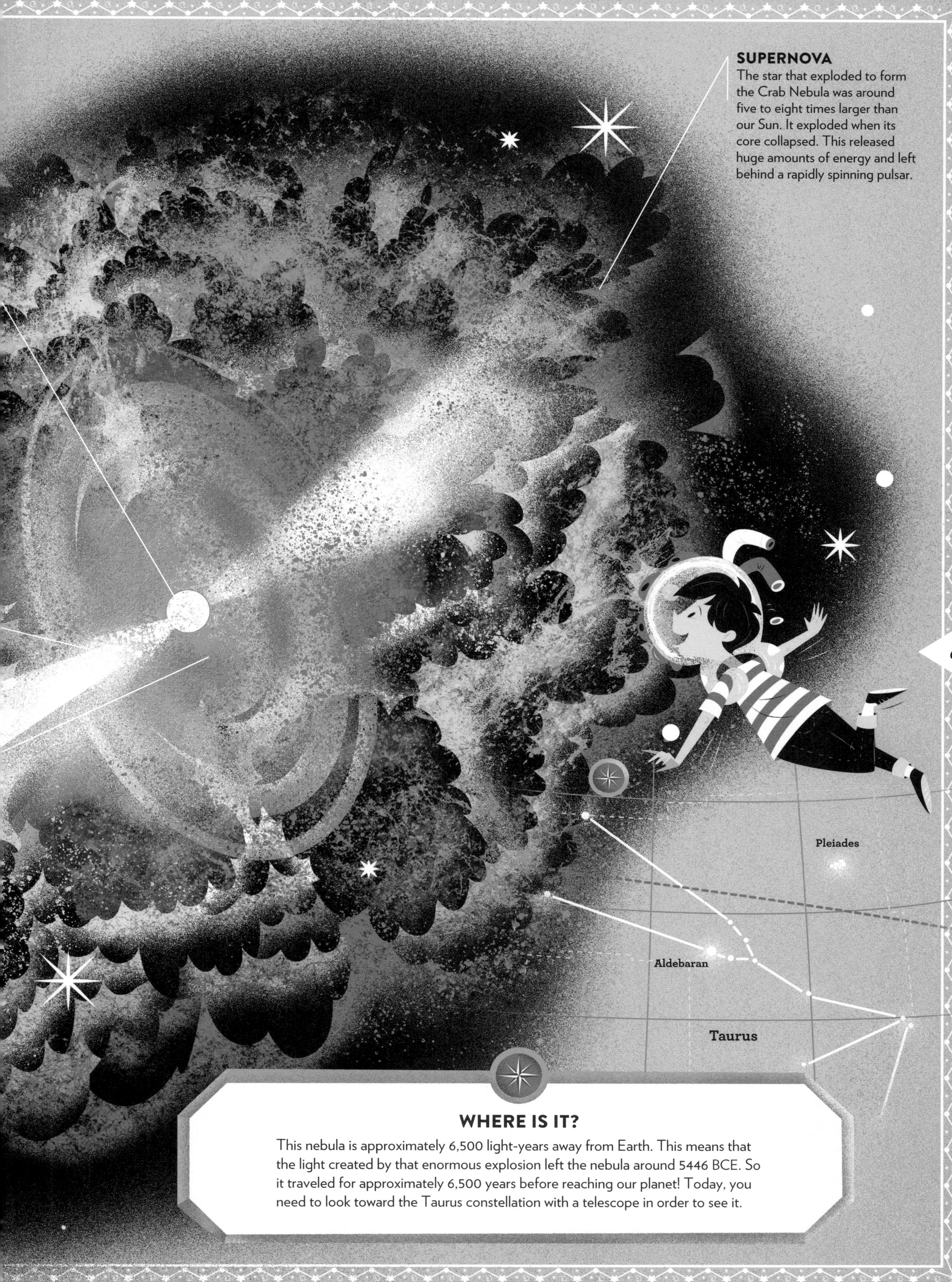

SUPERNOVA

The star that exploded to form the Crab Nebula was around five to eight times larger than our Sun. It exploded when its core collapsed. This released huge amounts of energy and left behind a rapidly spinning pulsar.

Pleiades

Aldebaran

Taurus

WHERE IS IT?

This nebula is approximately 6,500 light-years away from Earth. This means that the light created by that enormous explosion left the nebula around 5446 BCE. So it traveled for approximately 6,500 years before reaching our planet! Today, you need to look toward the Taurus constellation with a telescope in order to see it.

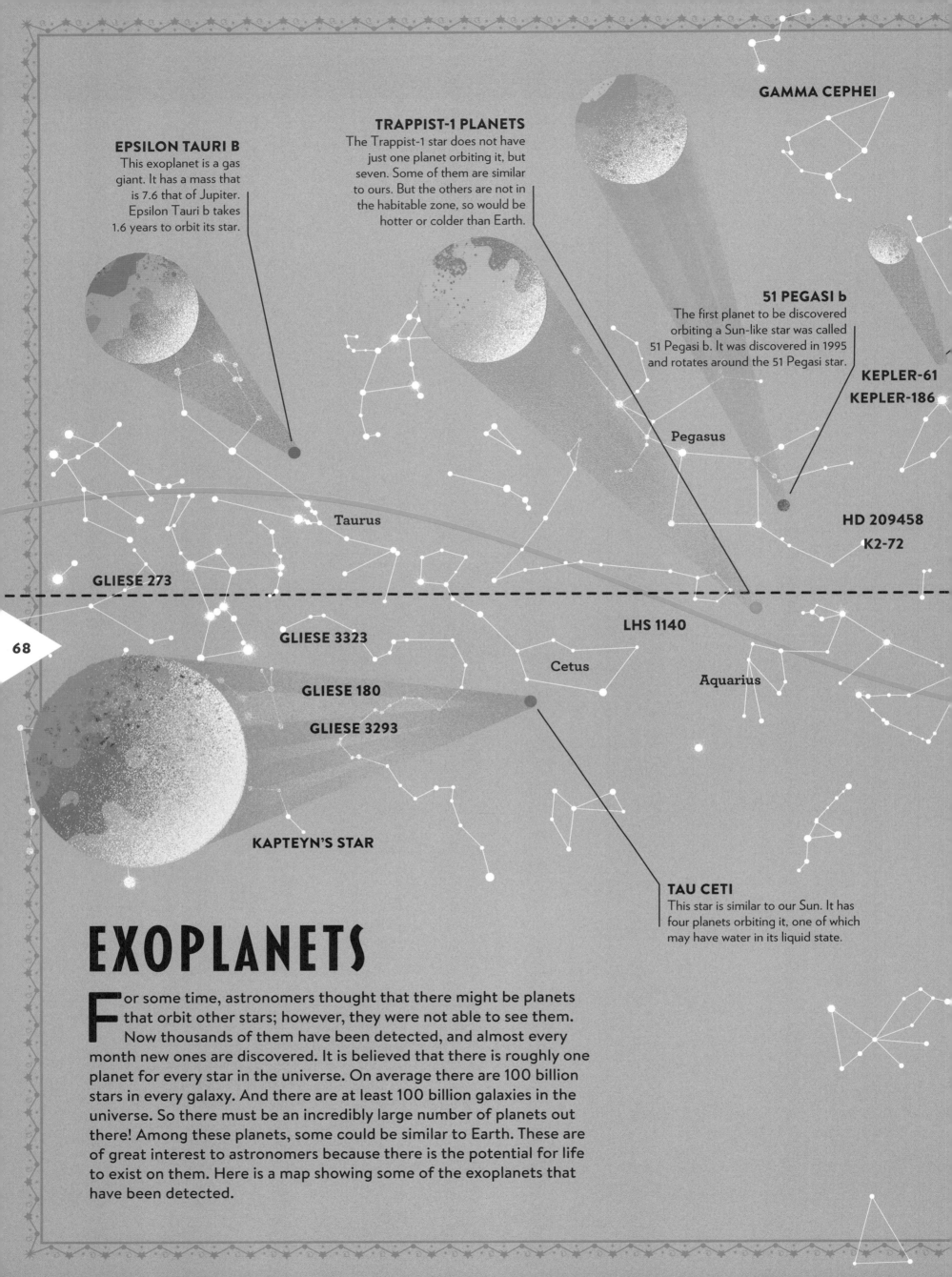

GAMMA CEPHEI

EPSILON TAURI B
This exoplanet is a gas
giant. It has a mass that
is 7.6 that of Jupiter.
Epsilon Tauri b takes
1.6 years to orbit its star.

TRAPPIST-1 PLANETS
The Trappist-1 star does not have
just one planet orbiting it, but
seven. Some of them are similar
to ours. But the others are not in
the habitable zone, so would be
hotter or colder than Earth.

51 PEGASI b
The first planet to be discovered
orbiting a Sun-like star was called
51 Pegasi b. It was discovered in 1995
and rotates around the 51 Pegasi star.

KEPLER-61
KEPLER-186

Pegasus

HD 209458
K2-72

Taurus

GLIESE 273

LHS 1140

68

GLIESE 3323

Cetus

Aquarius

GLIESE 180

GLIESE 3293

KAPTEYN'S STAR

TAU CETI
This star is similar to our Sun. It has
four planets orbiting it, one of which
may have water in its liquid state.

EXOPLANETS

For some time, astronomers thought that there might be planets
that orbit other stars; however, they were not able to see them.
Now thousands of them have been detected, and almost every
month new ones are discovered. It is believed that there is roughly one
planet for every star in the universe. On average there are 100 billion
stars in every galaxy. And there are at least 100 billion galaxies in the
universe. So there must be an incredibly large number of planets out
there! Among these planets, some could be similar to Earth. These are
of great interest to astronomers because there is the potential for life
to exist on them. Here is a map showing some of the exoplanets that
have been detected.

KEPLER-22b
Scientists think that the temperature on this planet is around 72°F (22°C). This is an ideal temperature for human beings. However, it is likely an ocean planet. So its surface would not be good for humans to live on.

ALIEN LIFE
Astronomers have discovered some planets that appear to be similar to ours. This means that there might be extraterrestrial life-forms out there. However, although there are planets that are a similar size, temperature, or distance from a sun, they have yet to find one that is exactly the same as Earth. Finding water on a planet increases the chance of the existence of life. So for this reason, many scientists are looking specifically for planets that have water in its liquid state.

KEPLER-1540
KEPLER-44
KEPLER-452
KEPLER-283

HD 189733 Ab
The blue color of this planet makes it look similar to the Earth. However, the color is not due to water, but to winds. They travel at 5,400 miles (8,700 km) per hour, carrying glass-like fragments, which reflect blue light.

ROSS 128 b
It is thought that this exoplanet is of a similar size to Earth and has a mild climate.

Cygnus

Virgo

K2-18
K2-9
K2-3

WOLF 1061

Libra

Sagittarius

GLIESE 581 b
There are several planets orbiting this star, including some that are thought to be very similar to the Earth.

GLIESE 667 C

GLIESE 682

Centaurus

GLIESE 422

SWEEPS-10
This planet has a very short orbit time; it only takes 10 hours to make a complete revolution.

PROXIMA CENTAURI B
The Alpha and Proxima Centauri system has three stars. Alpha Centauri A and Alpha Centauri B are the main stars. The third is called Proxima Centauri and has Proxima Centauri B orbiting around it. It is thought that there could be liquid water on this planet.

WHAT IS IT LIKE FOR HUMANS IN SPACE?

Humans are always looking for their next adventure.
Once we were able to see far into space, we decided that
we wanted to travel there. Scientists built rockets and
spaceships to send people out to explore the cosmos.
Now astronauts can venture to the International Space
Station, a space laboratory that is in orbit around the
Earth. There, they can discover what it's like to live in
space and can also conduct important experiments.

Here you can see the thickness of the layers in the atmosphere compared to each other. The thin white line is the troposphere.

WHERE DOES SPACE BEGIN?
There is some debate about the answer to this question. However, many scientists agree that space starts at a distance of 62 miles (100 km) above the Earth. Here, there is little atmosphere and planes cannot fly. This imaginary boundary between Earth's atmosphere and space is called the Kármán line.

EARTH'S ATMOSPHERE

In order to travel to outer space, astronauts need to escape the pull of Earth's gravity. Their spacecraft has to reach a certain speed called "escape velocity," which is 6.9 miles (11 km) per second. The spacecraft will then be going fast enough to shoot through the atmosphere and out into space. Earth's atmosphere has layers, and the layers change the higher up you go.

Mount Everest
20,029 feet
(8,848 m)

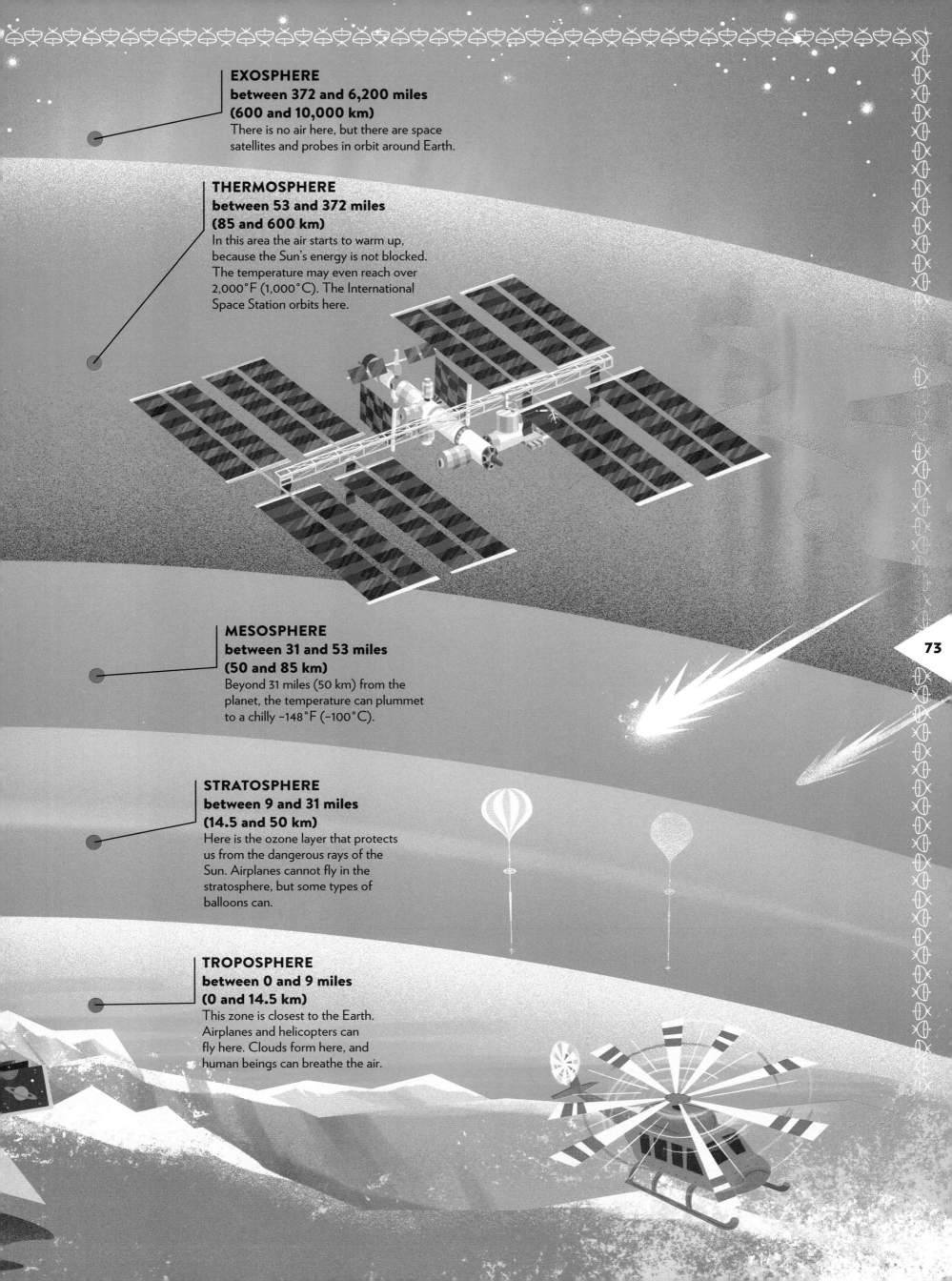

EXOSPHERE
**between 372 and 6,200 miles
(600 and 10,000 km)**
There is no air here, but there are space
satellites and probes in orbit around Earth.

THERMOSPHERE
**between 53 and 372 miles
(85 and 600 km)**
In this area the air starts to warm up,
because the Sun's energy is not blocked.
The temperature may even reach over
2,000°F (1,000°C). The International
Space Station orbits here.

MESOSPHERE
**between 31 and 53 miles
(50 and 85 km)**
Beyond 31 miles (50 km) from the
planet, the temperature can plummet
to a chilly –148°F (–100°C).

STRATOSPHERE
**between 9 and 31 miles
(14.5 and 50 km)**
Here is the ozone layer that protects
us from the dangerous rays of the
Sun. Airplanes cannot fly in the
stratosphere, but some types of
balloons can.

TROPOSPHERE
**between 0 and 9 miles
(0 and 14.5 km)**
This zone is closest to the Earth.
Airplanes and helicopters can
fly here. Clouds form here, and
human beings can breathe the air.

LARGE BINOCULAR TELESCOPE (LBT), USA
The LBT is on Mount Graham, in Arizona.

STONEHENGE, ENGLAND
This prehistoric monument is about 4,500 years old. It is aligned with the rising and setting Sun at certain times of the year.

MAUNA KEA, HAWAII
There are 13 telescopes located on Mauna Kea, a volcano in Hawaii.

ARECIBO OBSERVATORY, PUERTO RICO
This observatory looks like a large bowl. One of its jobs is to listen to the cosmos. It has been doing so for 50 years, hoping to hear an intelligent radio signal broadcast by some advanced form of alien life.

VERY LARGE TELESCOPE (VLT), CHILE
The VLT is formed by eight telescopes. It can be found in the Atacama Desert in the Chilean Andes. This telescope has gathered some of the most extraordinary images of space ever seen.

EXTREMELY LARGE TELESCOPE (ELT), CHILE
Not satisfied with the Very Large Telescope, astronomers are now working on the Extremely Large Telescope. Among other things, its aim is to study the atmosphere of exoplanets. Its construction is already under way on Cerro Armazones, which is also in the Chilean Andes.

ASTRONOMICAL OBSERVATORIES

Telescopes allow us to view space objects in astonishing detail. And by using telescopes we can even study things that are outside our solar system. In order to find such faraway objects we need special, super-large telescopes. We call these telescopes, and the buildings that house them, observatories. Many observatories are placed far from city lights and high up where the atmosphere is thin. From this vantage point, the view of the skies is much clearer than in cities.

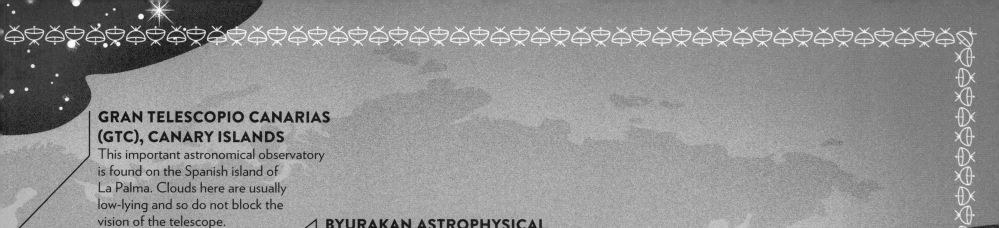

GRAN TELESCOPIO CANARIAS (GTC), CANARY ISLANDS

This important astronomical observatory is found on the Spanish island of La Palma. Clouds here are usually low-lying and so do not block the vision of the telescope.

BYURAKAN ASTROPHYSICAL OBSERVATORY (BAO), ARMENIA

The BAO can be found on Mount Aragats, in Armenia. It is thanks to this observatory that we know that stars are formed in groups.

LAMOST

FAST Radio Telescope

CHEOMSEONGDAE, SOUTH KOREA

This astronomical observatory was built of stone nearly 1,400 years ago. Amazingly, it is still intact. It has an opening in the roof that is very similar to that of modern observatories.

SOUTH AFRICAN LARGE TELESCOPE (SALT), SOUTH AFRICA

SALT is the largest optical telescope in the southern hemisphere, with a diameter of 36 feet (11 m). It is located 250 miles (400 km) from Cape Town.

SQUARE KILOMETRE ARRAY (SKA), SOUTH AFRICA AND AUSTRALIA

This gigantic radio telescope is being built in South Africa and Australia. It will point thousands of radio antennas into the starry sky.

Australian Astronomical Observatory

SOUTH POLE TELESCOPE (SPT), ANTARCTICA

There is even a telescope in Antarctica. It is not very easy to get to, but it is worth it. Because of the cold, the atmosphere there is very dry, so telescopes have a clear view of the sky.

HOW DO TELESCOPES WORK?

Telescopes capture light from objects and magnify it. Some, called optical telescopes, capture visible light, the kind we can see. Others capture radio waves, ultraviolet, or other kinds of light. The two types of telescopes that use visible light are called reflecting and refracting. A reflecting telescope catches light with a mirror and bounces it to the viewer. A refracting telescope catches light with a glass lens and bends it to the viewer. A radio telescope uses giant dishes or aerials to capture radio waves given off by faraway objects. It feeds the waves to a computer that turns them into an image.

WEATHER PREDICTION
These satellites monitor temperature, humidity, airflow, and the position of the clouds in the atmosphere. This information helps meteorologists predict the weather.

NAVIGATION
Many people use satellite navigation systems in their cars and on their mobile phones. These devices use a Global Positioning System (GPS) to pinpoint locations. GPS uses data from 30 satellites in different orbits around the Earth.

COMMUNICATION
These satellites are used when we make phone calls abroad or when we watch foreign television channels. They transmit signals between different parts of the world.

EARTH'S ARTIFICIAL SATELLITES

The International Space Station is one of many objects orbiting the Earth. The vast majority of other objects are satellites, which do everyday jobs such as transmitting television signals. Every dot you see on this map is an artificial satellite. There are approximately 2,000 working satellites in the air at any one time. However, the map shows more dots than this, because the satellites that no longer work continue to orbit the Earth. This creates trash, called space junk. Let's explore what some of the satellites do.

SCIENTIFIC EXPERIMENTS
Inside these satellites there are special conditions that you wouldn't find on Earth, for example reduced gravity. This is very useful for some scientific experiments.

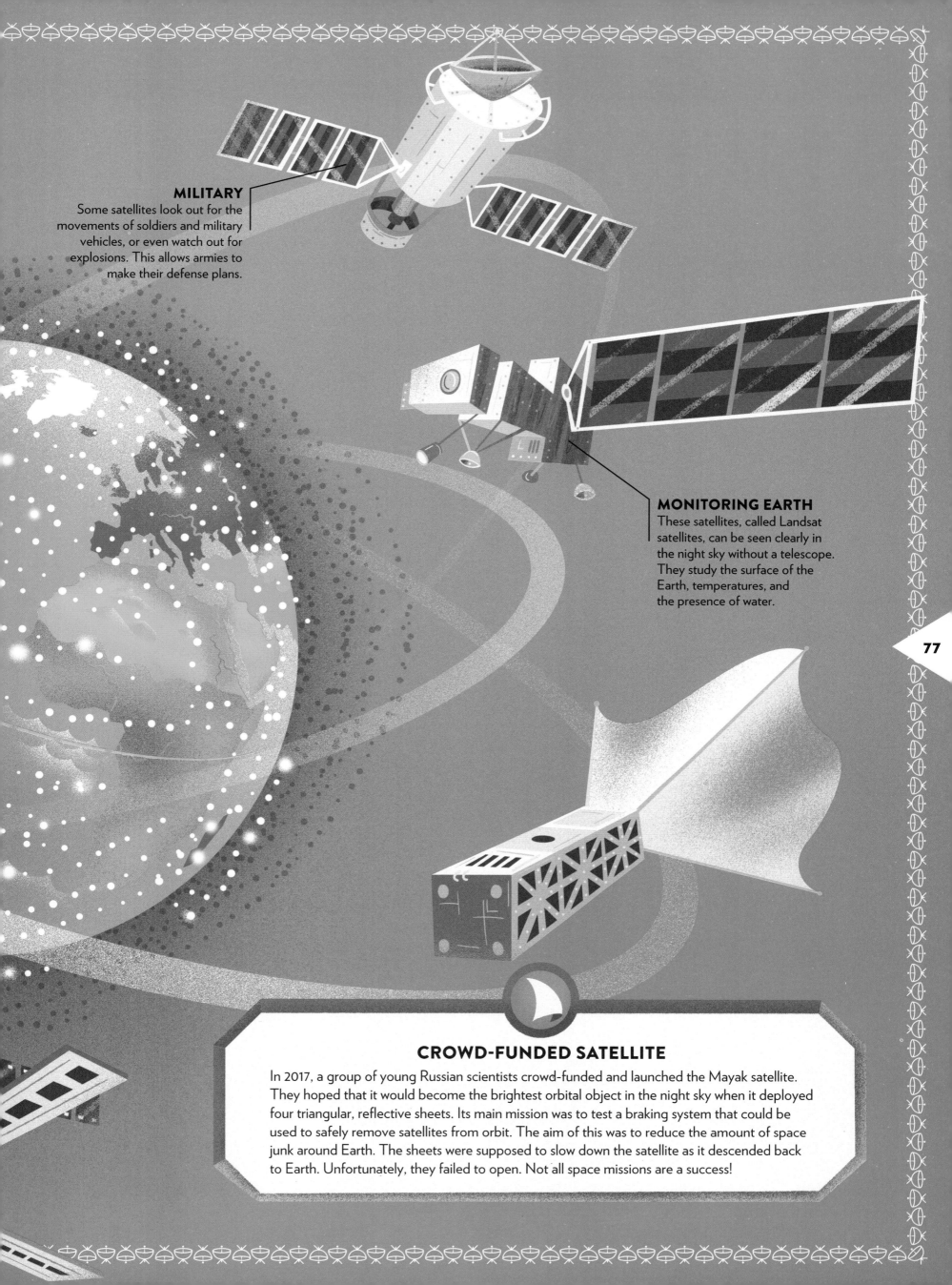

MILITARY
Some satellites look out for the movements of soldiers and military vehicles, or even watch out for explosions. This allows armies to make their defense plans.

MONITORING EARTH
These satellites, called Landsat satellites, can be seen clearly in the night sky without a telescope. They study the surface of the Earth, temperatures, and the presence of water.

CROWD-FUNDED SATELLITE

In 2017, a group of young Russian scientists crowd-funded and launched the Mayak satellite. They hoped that it would become the brightest orbital object in the night sky when it deployed four triangular, reflective sheets. Its main mission was to test a braking system that could be used to safely remove satellites from orbit. The aim of this was to reduce the amount of space junk around Earth. The sheets were supposed to slow down the satellite as it descended back to Earth. Unfortunately, they failed to open. Not all space missions are a success!

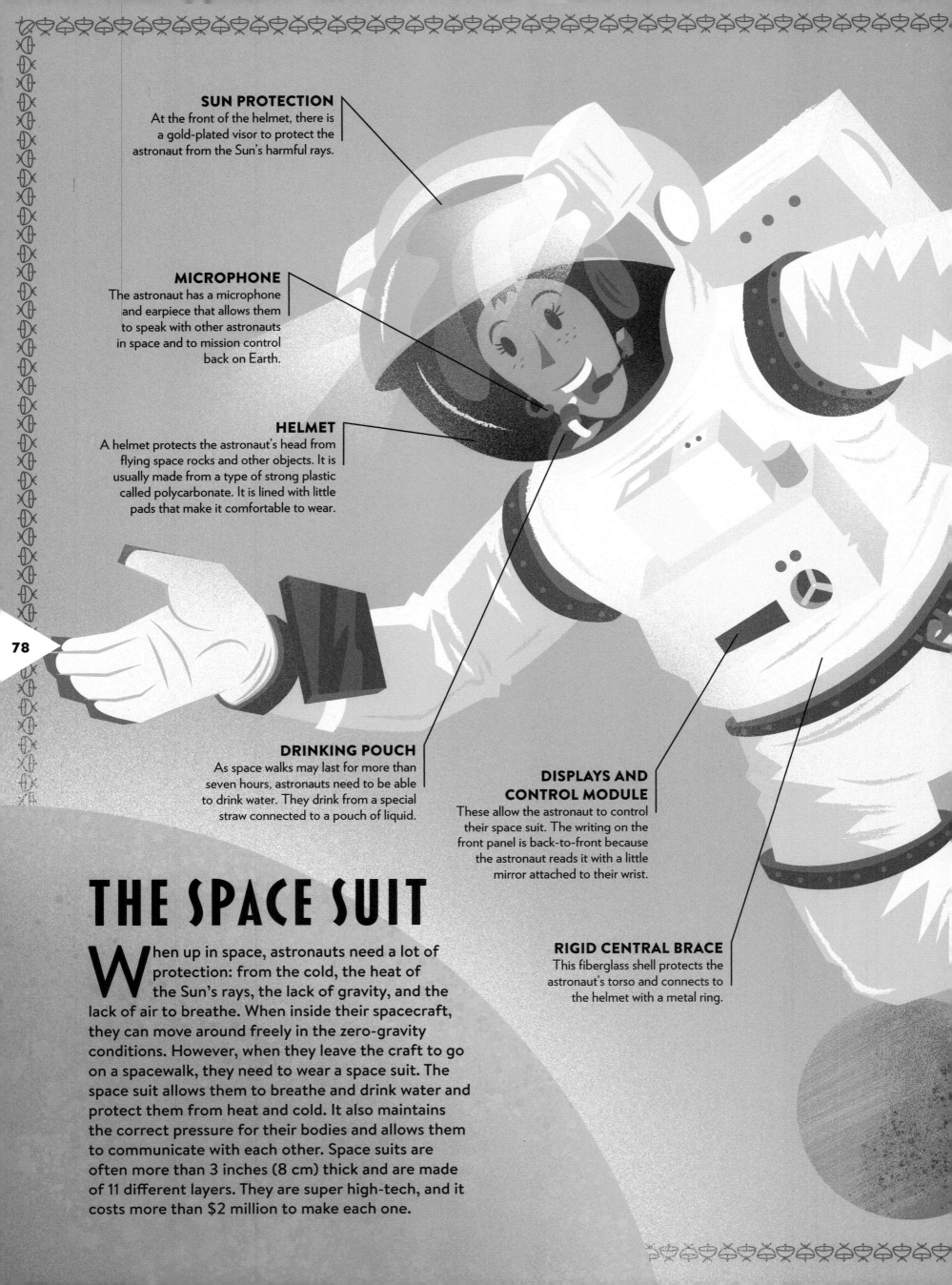

SUN PROTECTION

At the front of the helmet, there is a gold-plated visor to protect the astronaut from the Sun's harmful rays.

MICROPHONE

The astronaut has a microphone and earpiece that allows them to speak with other astronauts in space and to mission control back on Earth.

HELMET

A helmet protects the astronaut's head from flying space rocks and other objects. It is usually made from a type of strong plastic called polycarbonate. It is lined with little pads that make it comfortable to wear.

DRINKING POUCH

As space walks may last for more than seven hours, astronauts need to be able to drink water. They drink from a special straw connected to a pouch of liquid.

DISPLAYS AND CONTROL MODULE

These allow the astronaut to control their space suit. The writing on the front panel is back-to-front because the astronaut reads it with a little mirror attached to their wrist.

RIGID CENTRAL BRACE

This fiberglass shell protects the astronaut's torso and connects to the helmet with a metal ring.

THE SPACE SUIT

When up in space, astronauts need a lot of protection: from the cold, the heat of the Sun's rays, the lack of gravity, and the lack of air to breathe. When inside their spacecraft, they can move around freely in the zero-gravity conditions. However, when they leave the craft to go on a spacewalk, they need to wear a space suit. The space suit allows them to breathe and drink water and protect them from heat and cold. It also maintains the correct pressure for their bodies and allows them to communicate with each other. Space suits are often more than 3 inches (8 cm) thick and are made of 11 different layers. They are super high-tech, and it costs more than $2 million to make each one.

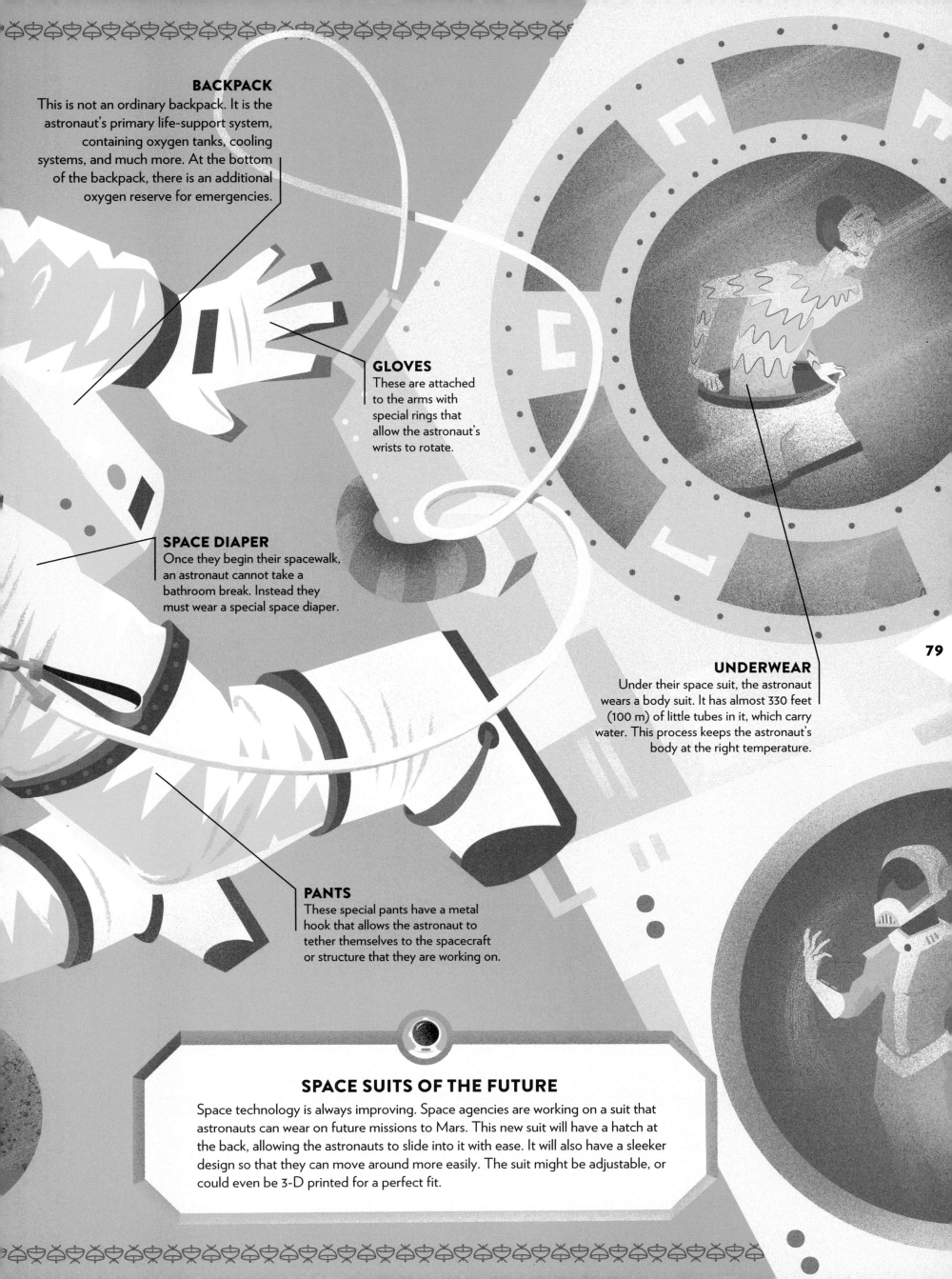

BACKPACK

This is not an ordinary backpack. It is the astronaut's primary life-support system, containing oxygen tanks, cooling systems, and much more. At the bottom of the backpack, there is an additional oxygen reserve for emergencies.

GLOVES

These are attached to the arms with special rings that allow the astronaut's wrists to rotate.

SPACE DIAPER

Once they begin their spacewalk, an astronaut cannot take a bathroom break. Instead they must wear a special space diaper.

UNDERWEAR

Under their space suit, the astronaut wears a body suit. It has almost 330 feet (100 m) of little tubes in it, which carry water. This process keeps the astronaut's body at the right temperature.

PANTS

These special pants have a metal hook that allows the astronaut to tether themselves to the spacecraft or structure that they are working on.

SPACE SUITS OF THE FUTURE

Space technology is always improving. Space agencies are working on a suit that astronauts can wear on future missions to Mars. This new suit will have a hatch at the back, allowing the astronauts to slide into it with ease. It will also have a sleeker design so that they can move around more easily. The suit might be adjustable, or could even be 3-D printed for a perfect fit.

ORBITAL MODULE
This round module is roughly the size of a large van and is where the crew lives while they are in orbit. It can connect to the space station.

SOYUZ CAPSULE
This is where the astronauts sit when the rocket is launched and also where they live while in space.

Antenna

Docking mechanism

Antenna

Camera

ROCKETS
These launch the spacecraft. When the vehicle reaches space, the rockets are turned off. Other rockets and smaller jets can be used to change direction. Most spacecraft can only go in one direction—up—but some can even use their rockets to land back on Earth.

This spaceship is leaving the launch pad. The rockets are ignited (turned on) and up it goes, through the atmosphere and beyond!

SPACECRAFT

By escaping Earth's gravity, spaceships can carry astronauts out beyond the atmosphere. Spaceships are usually divided into at least two parts. The capsule, or module, contains the scientific equipment and possibly the crew. The launch vehicle has rockets, which provide the energy needed to send the capsule into space. Let's have a closer look at a particular spacecraft, called Soyuz, and the rockets used to send it shooting into space.

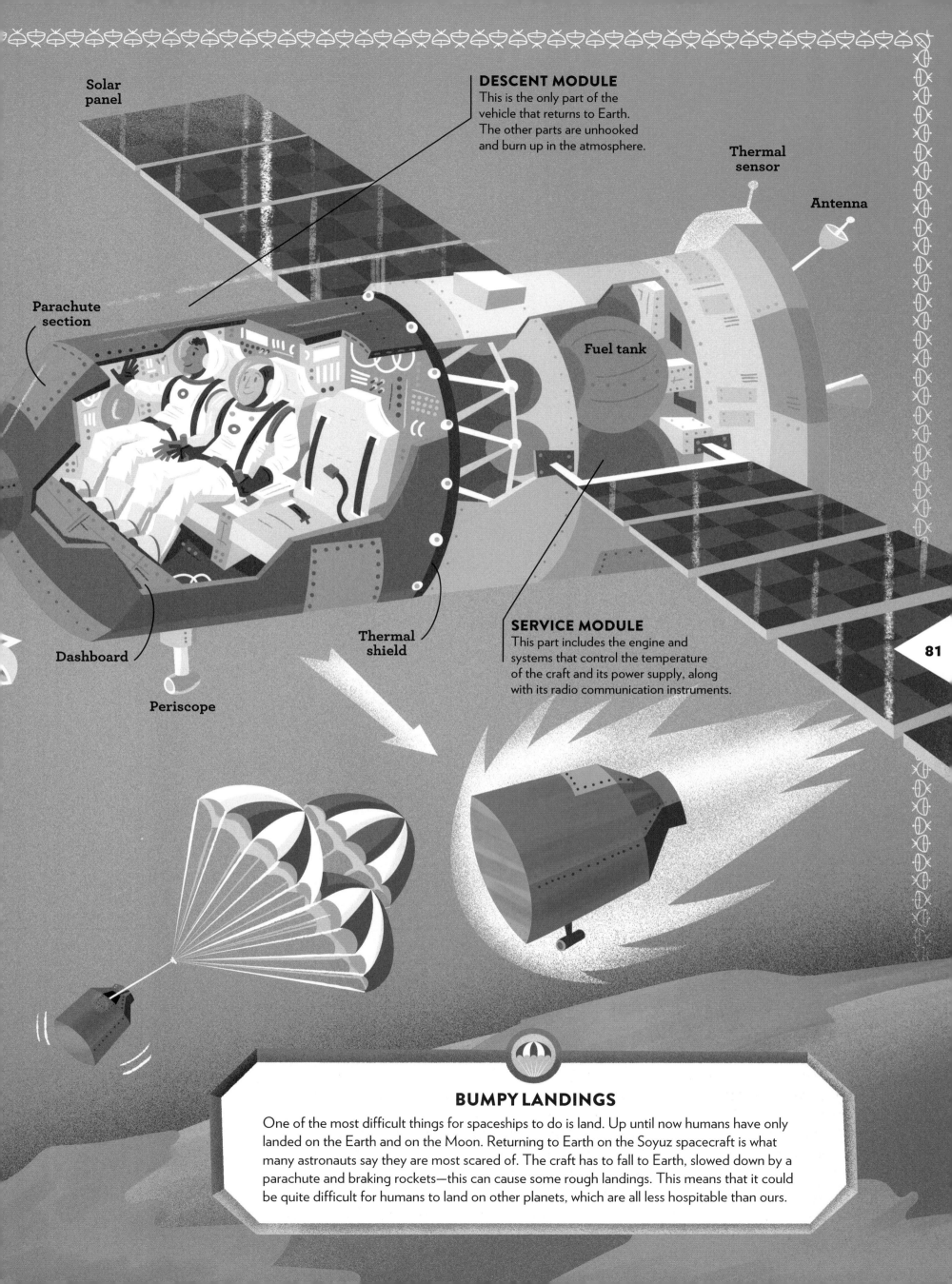

Solar
panel

DESCENT MODULE
This is the only part of the
vehicle that returns to Earth.
The other parts are unhooked
and burn up in the atmosphere.

Thermal
sensor

Antenna

Parachute
section

Fuel tank

Dashboard

Thermal
shield

Periscope

SERVICE MODULE
This part includes the engine and
systems that control the temperature
of the craft and its power supply, along
with its radio communication instruments.

BUMPY LANDINGS

One of the most difficult things for spaceships to do is land. Up until now humans have only
landed on the Earth and on the Moon. Returning to Earth on the Soyuz spacecraft is what
many astronauts say they are most scared of. The craft has to fall to Earth, slowed down by a
parachute and braking rockets—this can cause some rough landings. This means that it could
be quite difficult for humans to land on other planets, which are all less hospitable than ours.

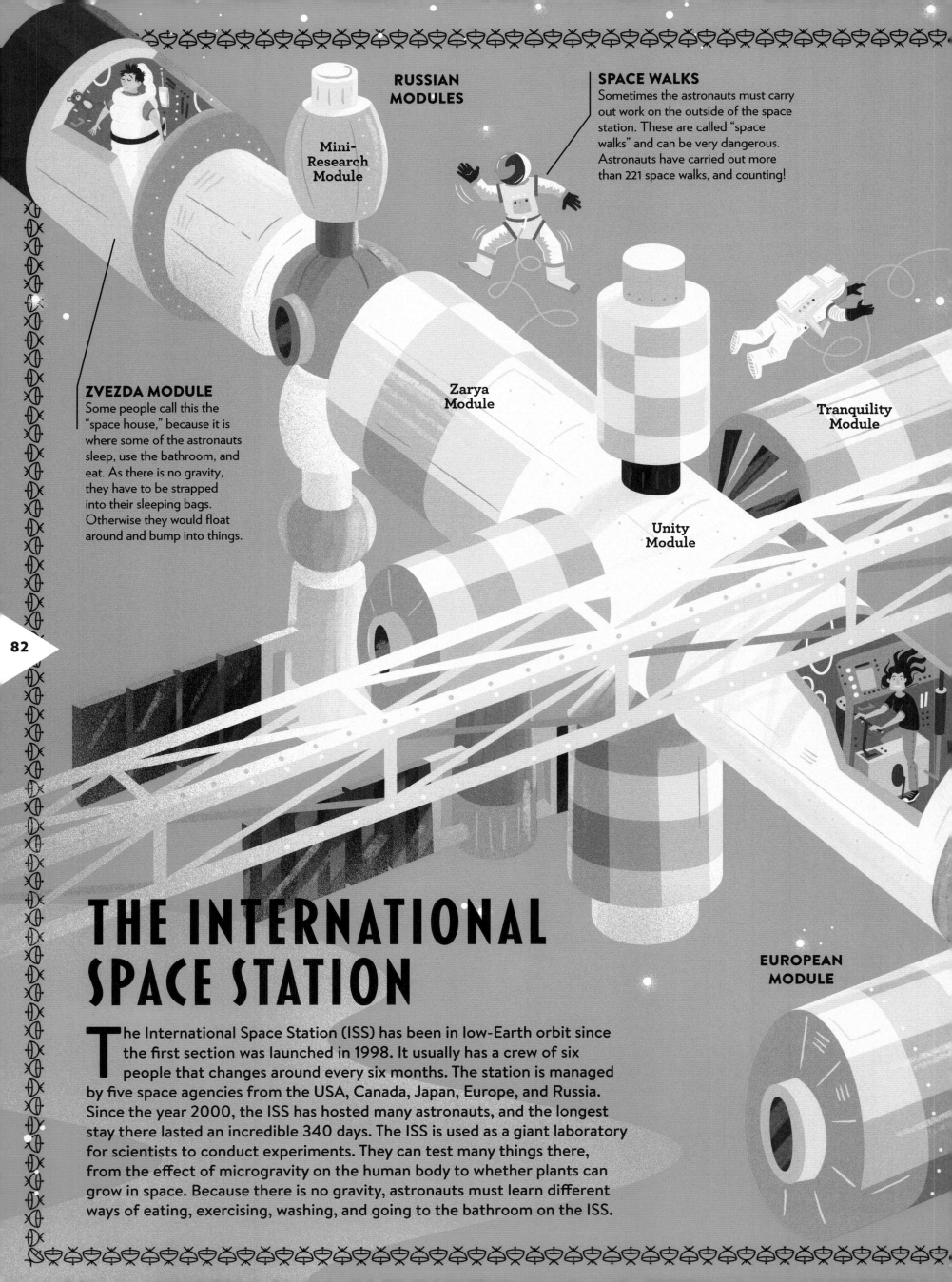

RUSSIAN MODULES

Mini-Research Module

SPACE WALKS
Sometimes the astronauts must carry out work on the outside of the space station. These are called "space walks" and can be very dangerous. Astronauts have carried out more than 221 space walks, and counting!

ZVEZDA MODULE
Some people call this the "space house," because it is where some of the astronauts sleep, use the bathroom, and eat. As there is no gravity, they have to be strapped into their sleeping bags. Otherwise they would float around and bump into things.

Zarya Module

Unity Module

Tranquility Module

THE INTERNATIONAL SPACE STATION

EUROPEAN MODULE

The International Space Station (ISS) has been in low-Earth orbit since the first section was launched in 1998. It usually has a crew of six people that changes around every six months. The station is managed by five space agencies from the USA, Canada, Japan, Europe, and Russia. Since the year 2000, the ISS has hosted many astronauts, and the longest stay there lasted an incredible 340 days. The ISS is used as a giant laboratory for scientists to conduct experiments. They can test many things there, from the effect of microgravity on the human body to whether plants can grow in space. Because there is no gravity, astronauts must learn different ways of eating, exercising, washing, and going to the bathroom on the ISS.

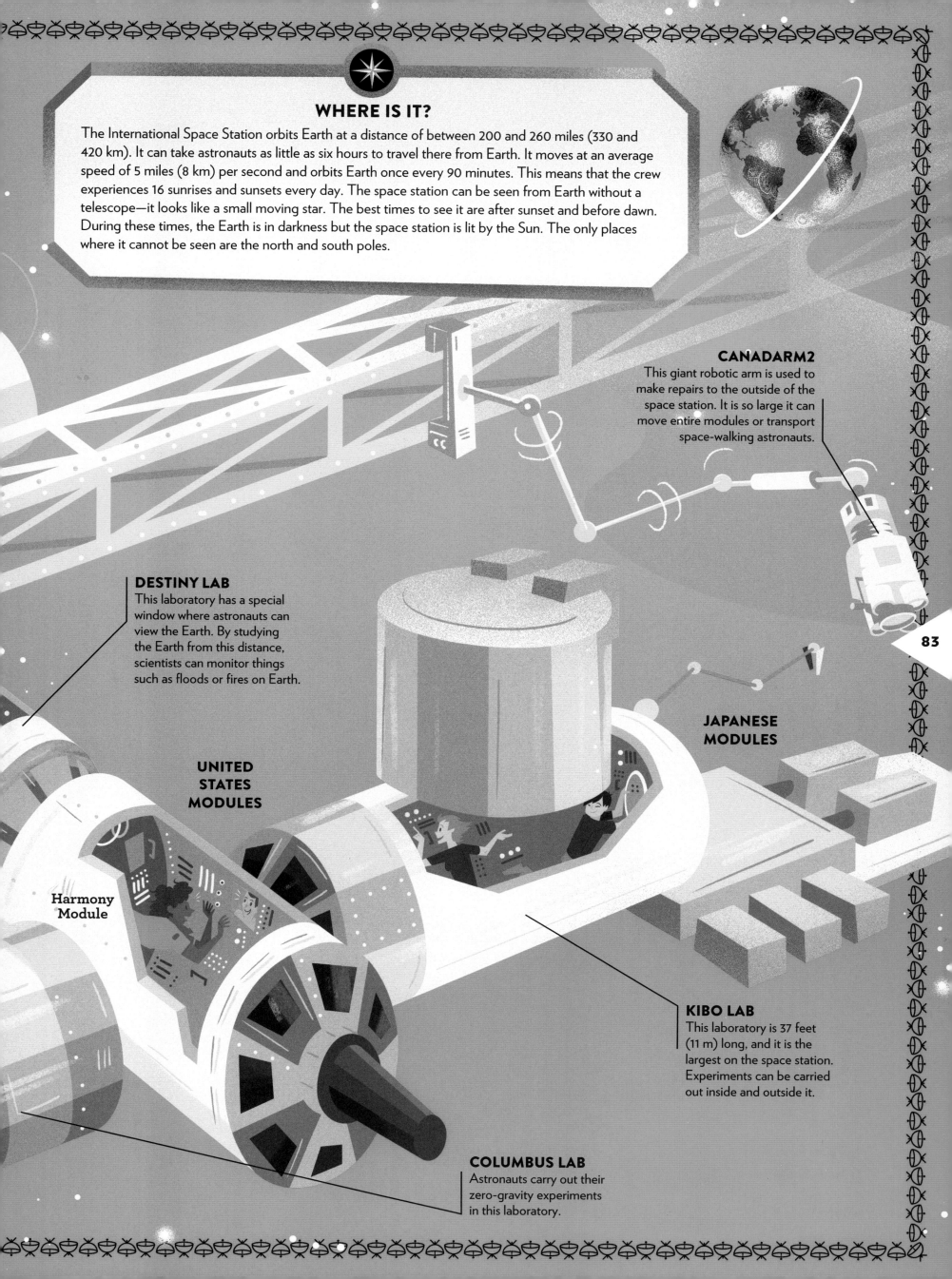

WHERE IS IT?

The International Space Station orbits Earth at a distance of between 200 and 260 miles (330 and 420 km). It can take astronauts as little as six hours to travel there from Earth. It moves at an average speed of 5 miles (8 km) per second and orbits Earth once every 90 minutes. This means that the crew experiences 16 sunrises and sunsets every day. The space station can be seen from Earth without a telescope—it looks like a small moving star. The best times to see it are after sunset and before dawn. During these times, the Earth is in darkness but the space station is lit by the Sun. The only places where it cannot be seen are the north and south poles.

CANADARM2
This giant robotic arm is used to make repairs to the outside of the space station. It is so large it can move entire modules or transport space-walking astronauts.

DESTINY LAB
This laboratory has a special window where astronauts can view the Earth. By studying the Earth from this distance, scientists can monitor things such as floods or fires on Earth.

JAPANESE MODULES

UNITED STATES MODULES

Harmony Module

KIBO LAB
This laboratory is 37 feet (11 m) long, and it is the largest on the space station. Experiments can be carried out inside and outside it.

COLUMBUS LAB
Astronauts carry out their zero-gravity experiments in this laboratory.

GLOSSARY

ASTEROID
Small rocky or metallic body that is in orbit around the Sun.

ASTRONOMER
Scientist who studies space.

ATMOSPHERE
Layer of gases that surrounds a planet.

AURORA
Colorful lights that occur in the sky. On Earth they often occur near the north and south poles and are caused by a reaction between the atmosphere and particles from the Sun.

AXIS
Imaginary line through the middle of something.

BLACK HOLE
Area of space that has such strong gravity that nothing, not even light, can escape it.

CELESTIAL
Relating to the sky.

COMET
Body made of dust and ice that orbits the Sun. Comets often release a cloud of gas and dust when they come close to our star, creating a characteristic "tail."

COSMONAUT
Russian astronaut.

CYCLONE
Violent storm.

DIAMETER
Length of a straight line if it were to pass directly through the center of something, from one side to another.

DWARF PLANET
A rounded celestial body that orbits a star but isn't big enough to have cleared out an orbit all its own.

ECLIPTIC
The path that the Sun appears to take across the sky.

EQUATOR
Imaginary line that runs around the center of the Earth (or other planet) at an equal distance from the north and south poles. The celestial equator is an imaginary line in the sky that is directly opposite Earth's equator.

EQUINOX
One of the two days in the year when day and night are the same length.

EXOPLANET
Planet that orbits a star outside of our solar system.

EXTRATERRESTRIAL
Something that exists on or comes from something (such as a planet or moon) other than Earth.

FIBERGLASS
Plastic that has been strengthened with glass fibers.

GALAXY
Enormous collection of stars, interstellar gas, dust, and solar systems that is held together by gravity.

GRAVITY
Force that attracts objects to each other.

HEMISPHERE
Half of a sphere. Earth's equator divides the Earth into the northern and southern hemispheres.

HOSPITABLE
Environment that is welcoming and suitable for living beings.

IMPACT CRATER
Depression or cavity on a planet, moon, asteroid, or comet that was caused by the impact of a meteorite or other object.

LATITUDE
Distance of a place from the equator.

LIGHT-YEAR
Distance that light travels in one year—approximately 6 trillion miles (9 trillion km).

LIQUID WATER
Water in its liquid form.

MAGNETIC FIELD
Area around a magnet or magnetic object in which there is a magnetic force.

MANEUVER
Skillfully move something.

METEORITE
Space rock that has traveled through the atmosphere of a planet or moon and landed on the surface.

METEOROLOGIST
Scientist who studies data from the atmosphere, the Sun, and the sea to make weather forecasts.

MOMENTUM
Force that something has while moving.

NEBULA
A cloud of interstellar dust and gas. Some nebulae form from the explosion of a dying star, and others are regions in which new stars form.

ORBIT
Path of an object around a star, planet, or moon.

PLATEAU
Large area of high, flat land.

PROBE
Spacecraft that travels into space without any humans on board.

ROVER
Remote-controlled vehicle.

SATELLITE
Object that moves around a bigger object. Moons are natural satellites.

STELLAR NURSERY
Area of space where gas and dust form new stars.

TECTONIC PLATE
Large, moving pieces of rock that make up a planet's outer layer.

TERRESTRIAL
Relating to planet Earth.

ZODIACAL CONSTELLATIONS
Constellations that lie along the ecliptic.

INDEX

A

Africa, southern *see San people*
Aldrin, Edwin "Buzz" 35
Alpha Centauri 6, 7, 9, 11, 13, 15, 69
Andromeda Galaxy 65
Armstrong, Neil 34, 35
asteroid 24, 32, 41, 43, 46, 50, 54, 56, 57
asteroid belt 24, 56, 57
astronaut 34, 35, 54, 61, 71, 72, 78, 79, 80, 81, 82, 83
astronomer 25, 30, 32, 39, 41, 48, 50, 51, 55, 57, 59, 62, 66, 68, 69, 74
atmosphere 22, 26, 27, 28, 32, 38, 40, 41, 42, 43, 44, 47, 50, 51, 52, 54, 61, 72, 73, 74, 75, 76, 81
aurora 47, 49, 51
axis 7, 29, 32

B

Beta Centauri 6, 7, 9, 11, 13, 15
black hole 21

C

Canis Major Galaxy 65
celestial equator 6, 7, 8, 9, 12
celestial pole 6, 9
Ceres 54, 56, 57
Charon 54, 55
China, ancient 12
cloud 23, 32, 46, 47, 50, 51, 52, 53, 64, 65, 73, 75, 76
comet 24, 25, 26, 32, 43, 46, 49, 50
constellation 6, 9, 10, 12, 14, 15, 60, 62, 67
corona 6, 10, 22, 40
cosmonaut 26
Crab Nebula 66, 67
crater 24, 32, 33, 38, 39, 40, 41, 42, 43, 44, 45, 46, 48, 49, 54, 55, 56, 57

D

deep space 59
deserts 28, 30
dust 24, 25, 31, 32, 47, 61, 62, 64, 65
dwarf planet 24, 25, 54, 56

E

Earth 6, 7, 8, 9, 12, 15, 18, 19, 21, 22, 23, 24, 26, 27, 28, 29, 30, 31, 32, 33, 34, 35, 37, 38, 39, 40, 41, 42, 43, 45, 46, 47, 48, 50, 52, 53, 54, 55, 57, 60, 61, 62, 65, 66, 67, 68, 69, 71, 72, 73, 76, 77, 78, 80, 81, 82, 83
ecliptic 9
equinox 9
escape velocity 72
exoplanet 63, 68, 69, 74
extraterrestrial 43, 69

G

Gagarin, Yuri 26
galaxies 18, 19, 59, 60, 61, 65, 68
Galilei, Galileo 48, 49, 50, 74
gas 22, 23, 25, 40, 46, 50, 52, 61, 62, 65, 66, 68
Goldilocks Zone 28
gravity 19, 21, 22, 24, 25, 26, 33, 46, 47, 48, 72, 76, 78, 80, 82, 83
Greeks, ancient 10, 12, 63

H

hemisphere 6, 7, 30, 38, 39, 40, 41, 42, 43, 56, 57, 65, 75
Hubble Deep Field 60
Hubble Space Telescope 60, 61, 73

I

International Astronomical Union 10
International Space Station 71, 73, 76, 82, 83

J

Jupiter 24, 25, 26, 27, 46, 47, 48, 49, 50, 53, 56, 68, 74

K

Kuiper Belt 25, 27

L

lander 27, 44, 45, 46
Large Magellanic Cloud 64, 65
legends 6, 12, 13
light pollution 30, 31
light-years 15, 18, 20, 21, 63, 64, 65, 67
lunar eclipse 32
lunar phases 33

M

Magellan, Ferdinand 64
magnetic field 26, 46, 50, 51
Mars 24, 26, 42, 43, 44, 45, 56, 79
Mercury 24, 26, 38, 39, 40, 42, 49
meteor 38
meteorite 41, 57
Milky Way (Galaxy) 7, 13, 14, 17, 20, 21, 30, 31, 61, 62, 64
mission (into space) 26, 27, 34, 35, 44, 45, 65, 77, 78, 79
momentum 24
moon 19, 24, 27, 38, 40, 42, 46, 47, 48, 49, 50, 51, 52, 53, 54, 55, 74
Moon, the (Earth's moon) 19, 26, 28, 29, 30, 32, 33, 34, 35, 38, 57, 74, 81
mountain 29, 32, 33, 38, 40, 41, 42, 43, 46, 48, 51, 54, 55, 56
myths 6, 10, 62

N

NASA 44, 61
nebula 62, 63, 64, 65, 66, 67

Neptune 24, 25, 27, 53
north pole 9, 28, 38, 42, 83
northern sky 6, 8, 10
nuclear fusion 23

O

observatory 55, 74, 75
Olympus Mons (Mars) 42, 43, 44
Oort Cloud 25
orbit 19, 24, 26, 32, 34, 46, 47, 48, 49, 50, 52, 53, 61, 63, 68, 69, 71, 73, 76, 77, 80, 82, 83
orbiter 44
Orion 6, 7, 8, 10, 11, 12, 14, 15, 20, 62, 63

P

planet 7, 9, 17, 19, 23, 24, 25, 26, 27, 28, 30, 37, 38, 39, 40, 41, 42, 43, 44, 45, 46, 47, 48, 49, 50, 51, 52, 53, 54, 55, 56, 59, 67, 68, 69, 74, 81
Pluto 25, 27, 54, 55, 56
Polaris (North Star) 6, 9, 10, 12, 13
probe 17, 26, 27, 33, 34, 35, 44, 45, 47, 73
pulsar 65, 66, 67

R

rings (planetary) 27, 47, 50, 51, 52, 53
robot 44, 83
rocket 80, 81
rover 34, 35, 44, 45, 46

S

Sagittarius Galaxy 65
San people 14, 15
satellite 24, 32, 44, 64, 73, 76, 77
Saturn 24, 25, 27, 50, 51
seasons 7
solar eclipse 29
solar system 9, 17, 24, 25, 26, 27, 28, 33, 34, 37, 38, 41, 43, 46, 49, 52, 53, 54, 59

south pole 28, 29, 33, 47, 75, 83
Southern Cross 7, 9, 11, 13, 15
Southern Pointers (Alpha and Beta Centauri) 6
southern sky 7, 8, 11, 15
Soyuz (spacecraft) 80, 81
space junk 76, 77
space suit 78, 79
space walk 78, 82, 83
spacecraft 4, 44, 45, 48, 50, 51, 72, 78, 79, 80, 81
star cluster 14, 59, 64, 65
star map 6
stars 5, 6, 7, 8, 10, 12, 14, 15, 18, 19, 20, 21, 22, 23, 30, 37, 61, 62, 63, 64, 65, 68, 69, 75
stellar nursery 21, 62
Sun 7, 8, 9, 17, 19, 20, 21, 22, 23, 24, 25, 26, 28, 29, 32, 33, 37, 38, 39, 40, 42, 46, 47, 48, 49, 50, 52, 53, 55, 56, 61, 63, 66, 67, 68, 69, 73, 74, 78, 83
supernova 65, 66, 67
Swigert, Jack 35

T

tectonic plate 28, 40
telescope 17, 18, 21, 30, 37, 47, 48, 53, 59, 60, 61, 62, 65, 66, 67, 73, 74, 75, 77, 83
terrestrial equator 8, 9
Tombaugh, Clyde 54

U

universe 4, 5, 17, 18, 19, 60, 68
Uranus 24, 25, 27, 52
Ursa Major (Plough) 6, 9, 10, 13, 60

V

Venus 24, 26, 39, 40, 41
volcano 29, 32, 40, 41, 42, 43, 46, 48, 74

Z

zodiacal constellations 9

SELECTED SOURCES

Albanese, Lara, 2017. *Costellazioni. Le stelle che disegnano il cielo*. Trieste: Editoriale scienza.

Albanese, Lara, 2018. *Atlante del cielo*. Milan: Jaca Book.

Albanese, Lara and Pacini, Franco, 2004. *Viaggio nell'Universo*. Milan: Jaca Book.

Albanese, Lara et al, 2012. *Storie dei cieli del mondo*. Rome: Sinnos.

Biedermann, Hans, 1991. *Enciclopedia dei simboli*. Milan: Garzanti.

Cattabiani, Alfredo, 1999. *Planetario: Simboli, miti e misteri di astri, pianeti e costellazioni*. Milan: Mondadori.

Chami, Felix A., 2008. *Evidence of Ancient African Beliefs in Celestial Bodies* in Holbrook, J., et al. *African cultural astronomy*. Berlin: Springer.

Fernandez, Julio A., et al, 2010. *Icy Bodies of the Solar System (IAU S263)*. Cambridge: Cambridge University Press.

Fountain, John W. and Sinclair, Rolf M., 1996. *Current Studies in Archaeoastronomy: Conversations Across Time and Space: Selected Papers from the Fifth Oxford International Conference at Santa Fe*. North Carolina: Carolina Academic Press.

Goldsmith, Donald, 2018. *Exoplanets, Hidden Worlds and the Quest for Extraterrestrial Life*. Cambridge, Massachusetts: Harvard University Press.

Hack, Margherita, 1993. *Alla scoperta del sistema solare*. Milan: Mondadori.

Heifetz, Milton and Tirion, Wil, 2006. *A Walk through the Heavens: A Guide to Stars and Constellations and Their Legends*. Cambridge: Cambridge University Press.

Heifetz, Milton and Tirion, Wil, 2012. *A Walk through the Southern Sky: A Guide to Stars and Constellations and Their Legends*. Cambridge: Cambridge University Press.

Hill Witt, Shirley and Steiner, Stan, 1992. *Scritti e racconti degli indiani-americani*. Milan: Jaca Book.

Holbrook, Jarita, et al., 2008. *African Cultural Astronomy: Current Archaeoastronomy and Ethnoastronomy research in Africa*. Cham: Springer.

Magli, Giulio, 2009. *Mysteries and Discoveries of Archaeoastronomy: From Giza to Easter Island*. New York: Copernicus Books (Springer Science + Business Media).

Magli, Giulio, 2013. *Architecture, Astronomy and Sacred Landscape*. Cambridge: Cambridge University Press.

Magli, Giulio, 2016. *Archaeoastronomy: Introduction to the Science of Stars and Stones*. Cham: Springer.

Medupe, R., 2009. *Stars in the African Skies: Earth and Beyond*. Cambridge: Cambridge University Press.

Milone, Eugene F. and Wilson, William J. F., 2016. *Solar System Astrophysics: Background Science and the Inner Solar System*. Cham: Springer.

Pankenier, David, et al., 2008. *Archaeoastronomy in East Asia : Historical Observational Records of Comets and Meteor Showers From China, Japan, and Korea*. Amherst, New York: Cambria Press.

Ries, Julien, 2005. *Il mito. Il suo linguaggio e il suo messaggio attraverso le civiltà*. Milan: Jaca Book.

Romano, Giuliano, 1999. *I Maya e il cielo. Astronomia, cosmologia e matematica maya*. Pauda: CLEUP.

Ruggles, Clive L. N., 2011. *Archaeoastronomy and Ethnoastronomy: Building Bridges between Cultures*. Cambridge: Cambridge University Press.

Sagan, Carl, 2000. *The Cosmic Connection: An Extraterrestrial Perspective*. Cambridge: Cambridge University Press.

Schilling, Govert, 2019. *Constellations: The Story of Space Told Through the 88 Known Star Patterns in the Night Sky*. New York: Black Dog & Leventhal Publishers Inc.

Selin, Helaine, 2008. *Encyclopaedia of the History of Science, Technology, and Medicine in Non-Western Cultures*. Dordrecht: Kluwer Academic.

https://www.eso.org/public/

http://www.exoplanetkyoto.org/

https://www.iau.org/

https://www.nasa.gov/

https://www.noao.edu/

https://www.rmg.co.uk

https://www.raritanval.edu/sites/default/files/aa_PDF%20Files/6.x%20Community%20Resources/6.4.5_SD.7.AfricanMythology.pdf

https://www.raritanval.edu/sites/default/files/aa_PDF%20Files/6.x%20Community%20Resources/6.4.5_SD.12.ChineseLegends.pdf

https://pubs.usgs.gov/sim/3316/downloads/sim3316_sheet2_lo_res.pdf

https://www.nationalgeographic.com/science/space/space-exploration/moon-exploration/

http://luna1.diviner.ucla.edu/~dap/pubs/019.pdf

https://www.lpi.usra.edu/resources/venus_maps/1562_1/I-1562_1of2_300.jpg

https://www.newscientist.com/article/dn7039-pack-ice-suggests-frozen-sea-on-mars/

https://www.ucsusa.org/resources/satellite-database

https://www.asc-csa.gc.ca/eng/iss/canadarm2/about.asp

https://www.issnationallab.org/about/iss-timeline/

What on Earth Books is an imprint of What on Earth Publishing
The Black Barn, Wickhurst Farm, Tonbridge, Kent TN11 8PS, United Kingdom
30 Ridge Road Unit B, Greenbelt, Maryland, 20770, United States

First published in Italy under the title Mappe Spaziali © Dalcò Edizioni S.r.l.,
Via Mazzini 6, 43121 Parma
www.dalcoedizioni.it

First published in English in 2020 by What on Earth Books

Translation © 2020 What on Earth Publishing Ltd
Text: Lara Albanese
Illustrations: Tommaso Vidus Rosin

Staff for this edition:
Katy Lennon, Editor
Andy Forshaw, Art Director
Daisy Symes, Designer
Stuart Atkinson, Subject Consultant
Rose Blackett-Ord, Fact Checker

Library of Congress Cataloging-in-Publication Data available upon request

ISBN: 978-1-9129205-6-3

Printed in China

1 3 5 7 9 10 8 6 4 2

whatonearthbooks.com